Drawing D...

Written & Illustrated by Belinda Willson

Design & Layout by Jason Willson

FOREWORD

Before commencing any drawing, it is recommended you have at least three different soft pencils, an eraser and a sharpener. 2B, 4B and 6B pencils are preferred and can be purchased from most Art Suppliers and Newsagents.

This book has been designed to encourage the development of good drawing and improve the artist's perception. The studies begin at a relatively easy standard, using a basic four step process to systematically explain the method. The steps are gradually reduced as it is expected the artist will be more aware and techniques, better retained.

As the book progresses, you are encouraged to adopt a more independent approach, thus further enhancing these newly acquired skills.
A series of hints and instructions are included for each illustration.

Good Luck on your path to better drawing!

ISBN: 1 86476 295 0

Copyright © Axiom Publishing, 2004.
Unit 2, 1 Union Street, Stepney, South Australia, 5069.

This book is copyright. Apart from any fair dealing for the purpose of private study, research, criticism or review, as permitted under the Copyright Act, no part may be reproduced by any process without written permission. Enquiries should be made to the publisher.

Axiom Australia
www.axiompublishers.com.au

Printed in Malaysia

Drawing Dogs

PHYSICAL CHARACTERISTICS

Comparative size- **30 inches:** Great Dane. **15 inches:** Greyhound. **10 inches:** Silky Terrier.

OBSERVATION DETAILS:

Dogs come in many different shapes and sizes determined by the structure of the head, body and legs. Of course, colour and length of hair type play their parts in adding to that variation, but just for the moment let us look at the actual structure of the dog. Firstly the head, revealing two basic shapes, a narrow head with a long snout and a wide head with a short snout. Ears may be long or short, erect or down. The neck is significant depending on the breed. The body of all dogs contains 27 bones from the skull to the start of the tail. The legs and paws are used for standing, moving, scratching, and in some breeds, digging. All these structural differences are seen in the wide variety shown within this book. This stated, we should always recognise the variations between breeds, mostly created through human intervention with practical usage being the main intention, i.e. working dogs such as border collies and spaniels, toy dogs such as the chihuahua, fighting dogs such as the bull terrier, and guard dogs in the case of the doberman.

Drawing Dogs

SKELETAL

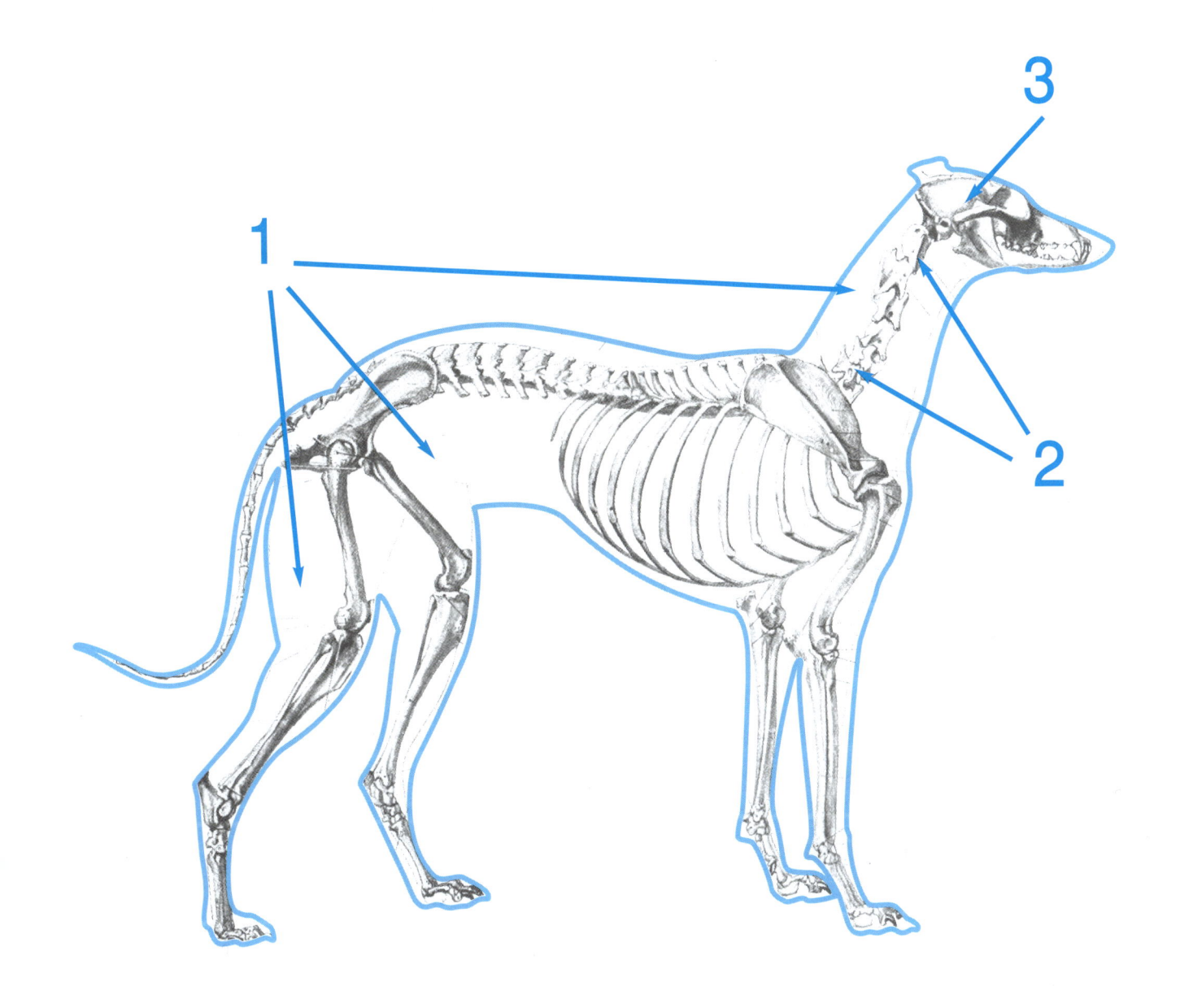

OBSERVATION DETAILS:

The skeletal frame of the dog is strong providing very good protection to vital organs and excellent anchors for its complex muscle system.

1. Notice the bare areas inside the body framework, taken up largely by muscle tissue, supporting and strengthening the skeleton of the dog.
2. The neck bones of the dog are strong and flexible. They have an inter-connective quality helping to provide the agility needed by the dog in its wide range of head and neck movements.
3. The head of the dog is largely bone mass, and almost the entire shape of the head is determined by the skeletal frame within.

Drawing Dogs

ANATOMY

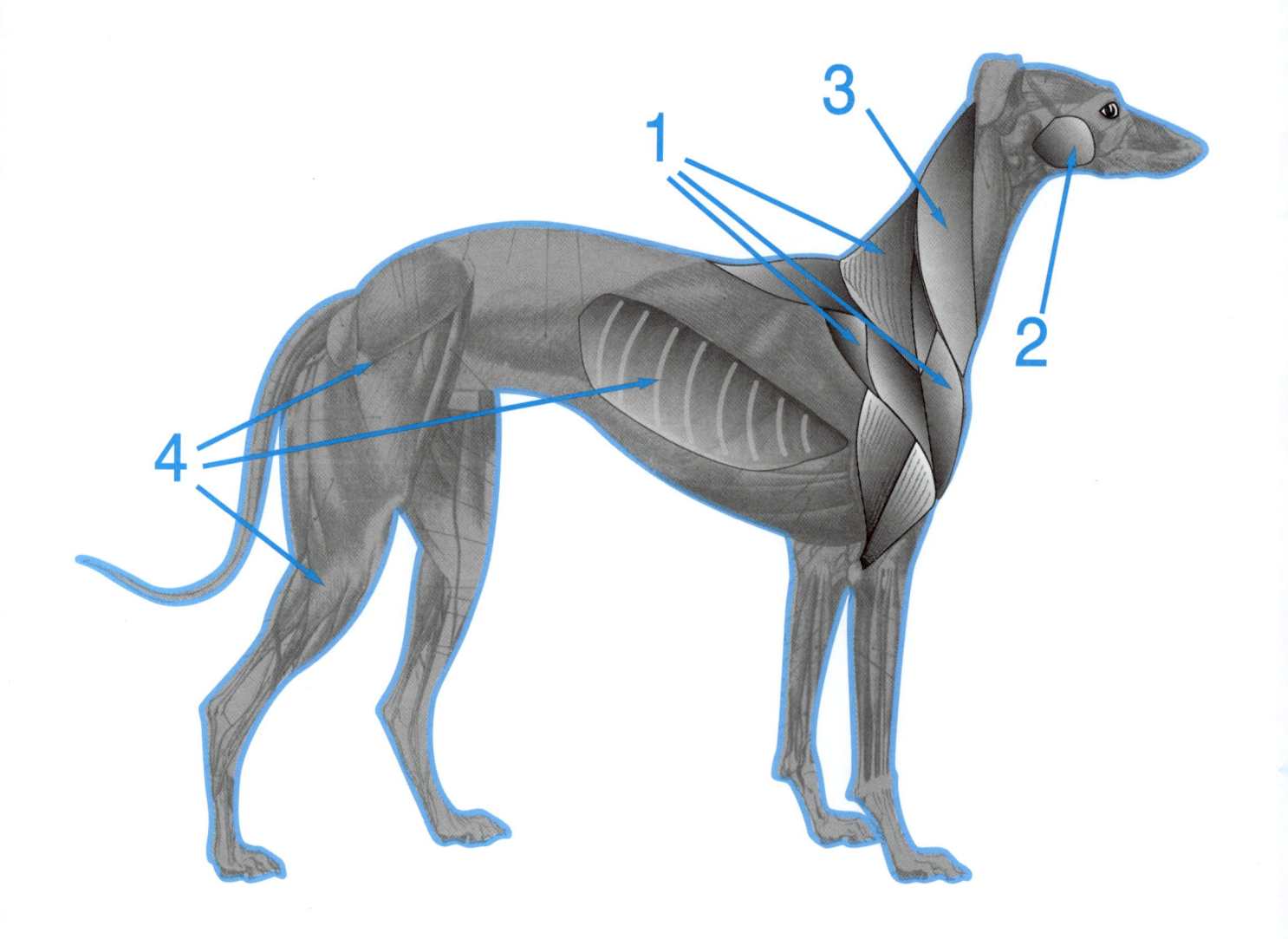

OBSERVATION DETAILS:

By having a broad awareness of the main muscular system the illustrator can more fully understand the movement of dogs. When a muscle contracts or relaxes it pulls on the bone to which it is attached creating movement. Every muscle is paired with another which exerts an opposite force allowing the dog to engage in a wide variety of complex movements. The muscles of the dog are very strong giving power and speed.

1. Notice the complex muscle structure around the shoulders and neck areas.
2. The jaw muscles are rather large and pronounced.
3. The size of the muscular planes are an indication of the strength needed in that area of the anatomy to support the surrounding structure of the body.
4. The dog has chiselled body lines, a robust frame and a firm foothold. The rib cage is long and contoured to support the large stomach and intestines of the dogs' digestive system.

Drawing Dogs

PROFILE

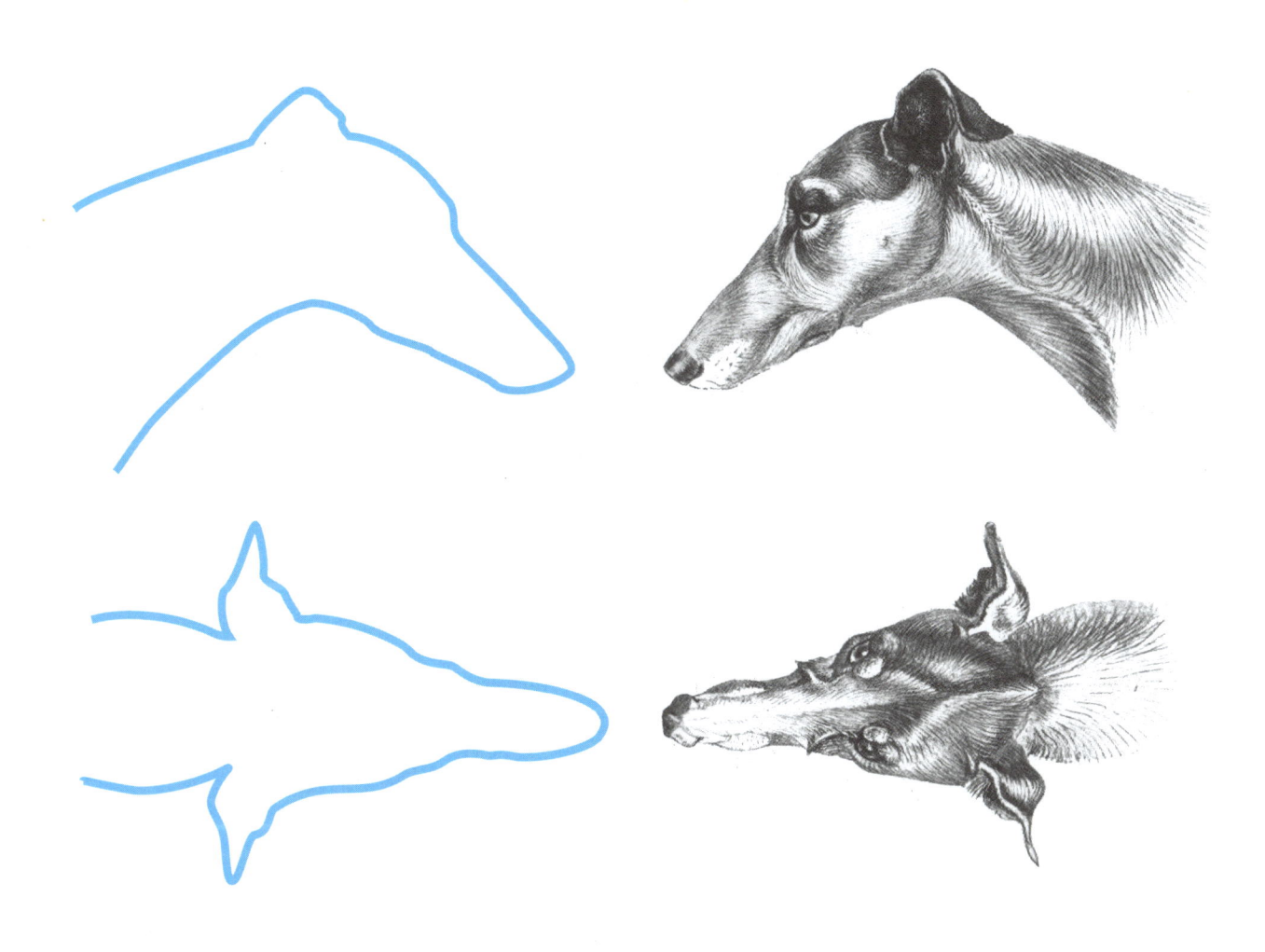

OBSERVATION DETAILS:
These two profiles show the outline form which is the first stage for this style of drawing. Once the angle of the profile is set, the detailing of the shadows and highlights can be included. In this case there are no extreme angles to the profile other than a direct side-on and direct downward view. For this reason the main details giving a pronounced effect to the profile are the darkest shadow areas. A great way to start is with the main dark areas, progressing along to the finer shadow areas and lines. Remember to leave some clear white areas as these make the shadows appear deeper and more defined.

Drawing Dogs

PUG

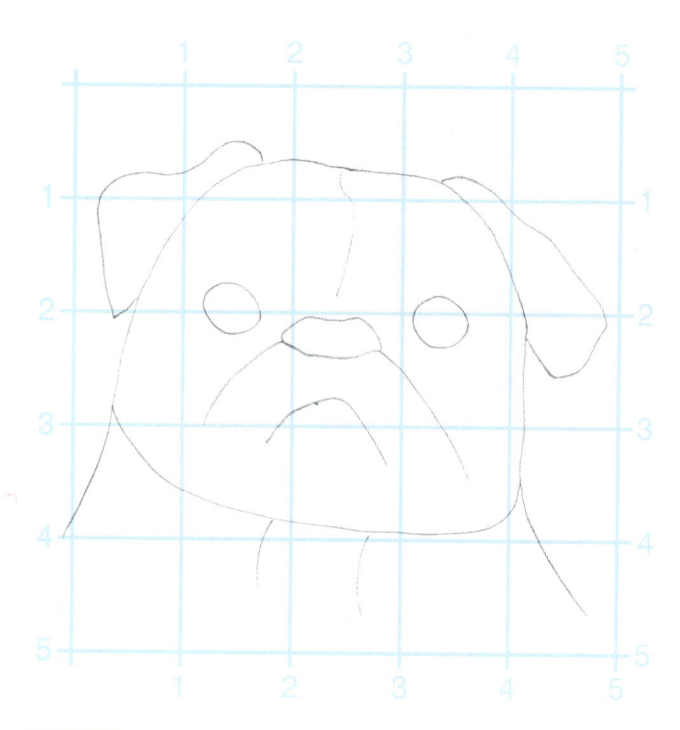

STEP 1:
On your own piece of paper, begin by very lightly drawing a twenty-five square grid using a ruler. A standard 2B pencil is ideal to draw basic circles and lines, as well as the main shapes of the finished sketch. Use the grid to help create accurate proportions.

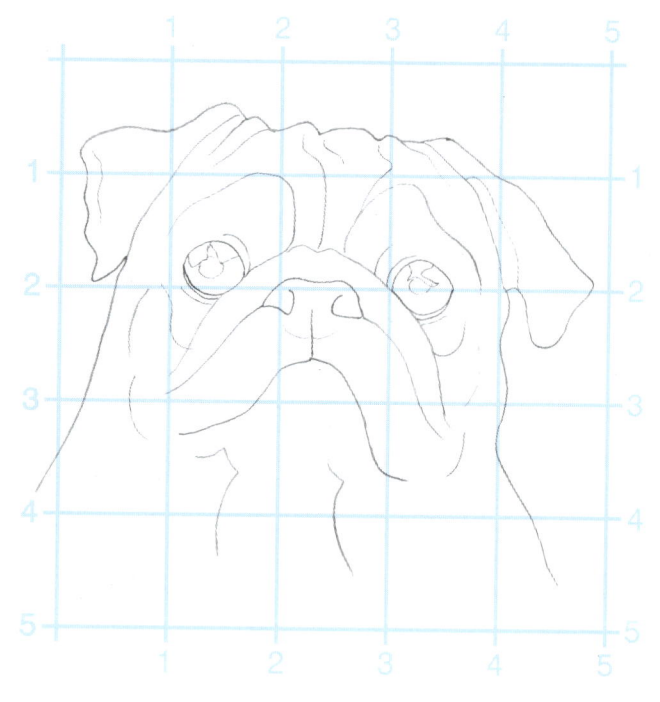

STEP 2:
Lightly sketching, follow the basic shapes you have just created and develop the outline of the image and its features. Still focusing on proportions and accuracy.

STEP 3:
When satisfied with your outlines, use an eraser to tidy any unnecessary lines or mistakes.

STEP 4:
Using a 4B and a 6B pencil to lightly render the image, copy the techniques shown in the example and read the observation details to help achieve an accurate result.

Drawing Dogs

OBSERVATION DETAILS:

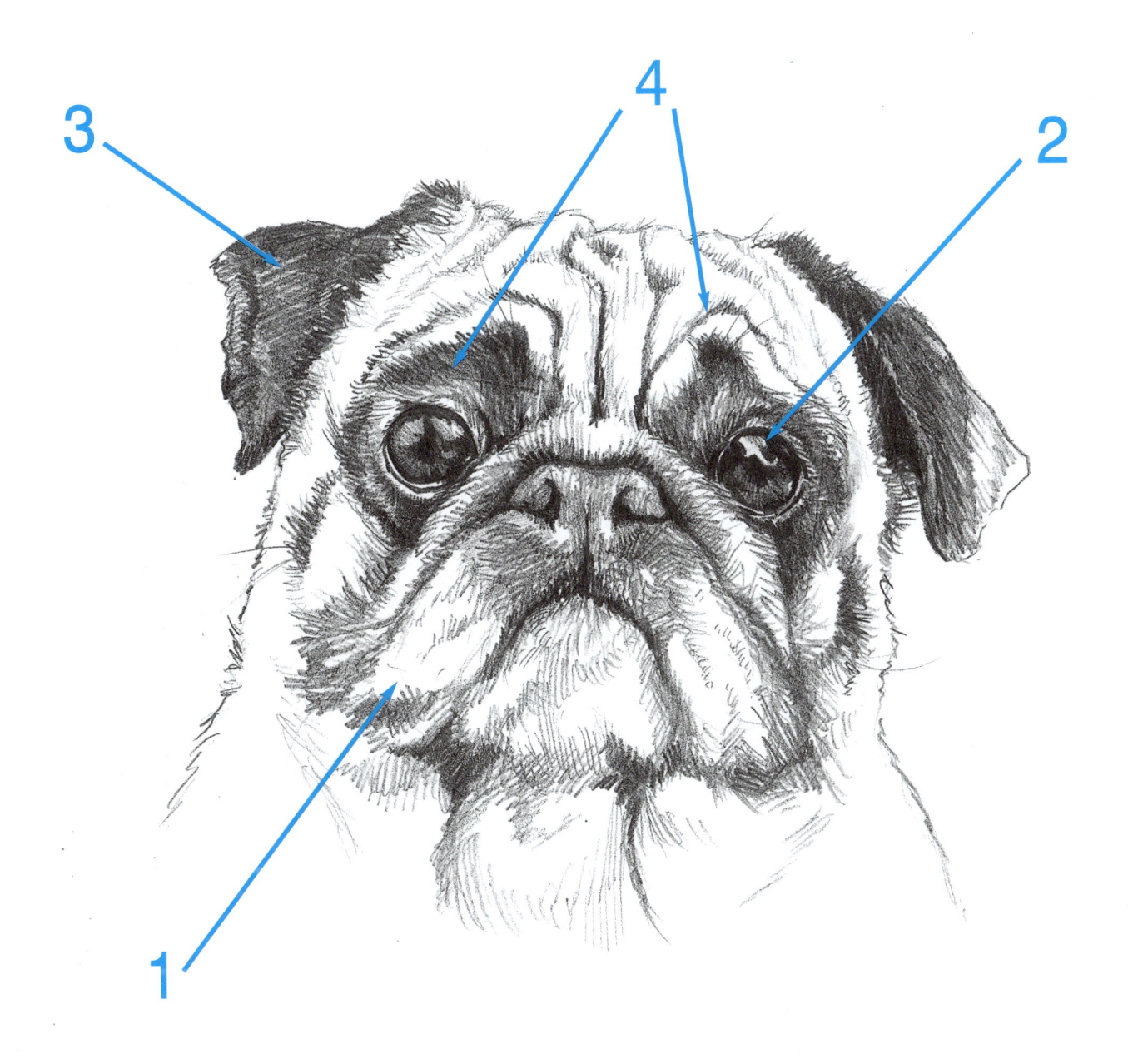

1. To draw more attention to the facial features and create greater highlights on the Pug's fur, allow the white paper to come through within the drawing. This provides contrast to the darker areas.
2. When drawing the eyes, it is important to keep the illusion of wetness and shine. Shade carefully around the reflections. When the rest of the eye is completed, the darker features can be finished with a 2B pencil, only lightly does it.
3. For effectively darker shadows, use your 6B pencil. This is a soft pencil and there's no need to press too firmly, otherwise damage or denting of the paper may occur.
4. Eyes seriously influence facial expression, as eyebrows do on a human face. To achieve effective colouring above the eye, wrinkles should be shown as raised, giving that classic Pug look.

Drawing Dogs

MIXED BREED 1

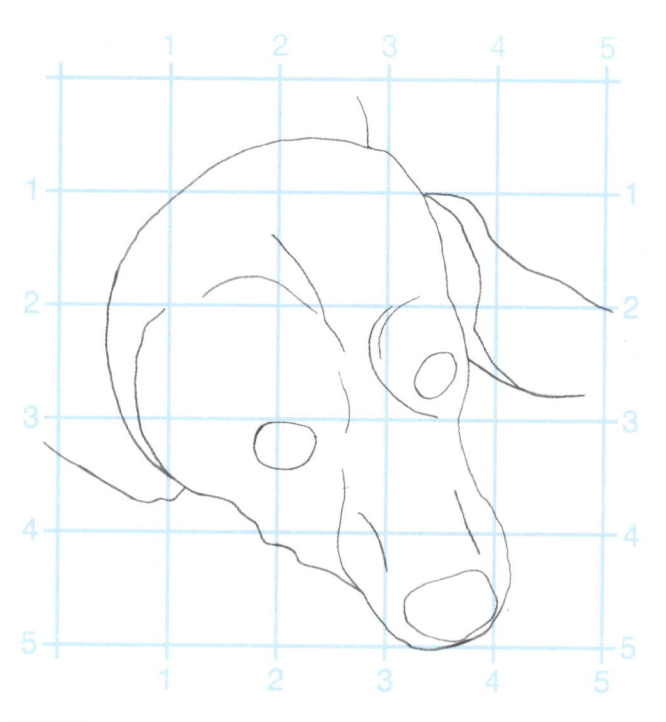

STEP 1:
On your own piece of paper, begin by very lightly drawing a twenty-five square grid using a ruler. A standard 2B pencil is ideal to draw basic circles and lines, as well as the main shapes of the finished sketch. Use the grid to help create accurate proportions.

STEP 2:
Lightly sketching, follow the basic shapes you have just created and develop the outline of the image and its features. Still focusing on proportions and accuracy.

STEP 3:
When satisfied with your outlines, use an eraser to tidy any unnecessary lines or mistakes.

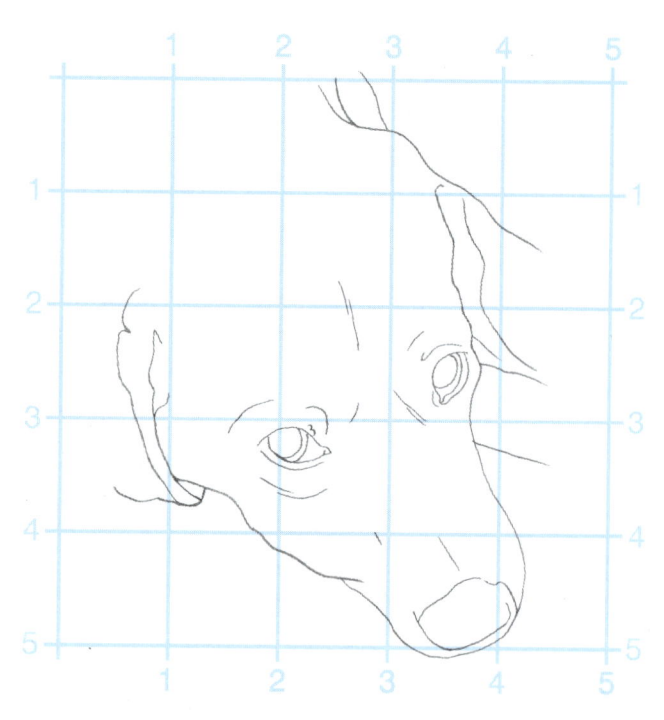

STEP 4:
Using a 4B and a 6B pencil to lightly render the image, copy the techniques shown in the example and read the observation details to help achieve an accurate result.

Drawing Dogs

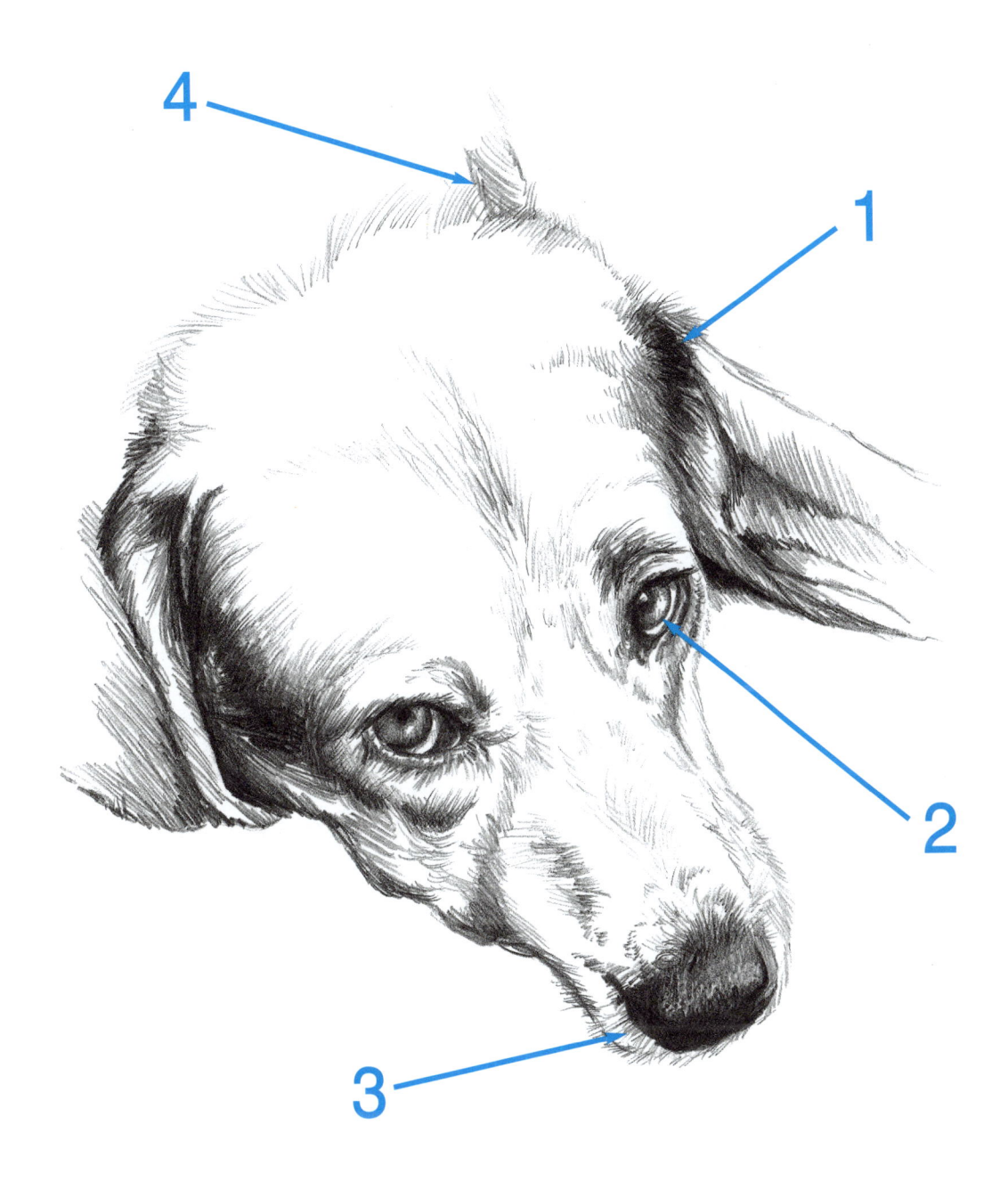

OBSERVATION DETAILS:

1. Focusing on the shadows, gradually build on these by beginning softly, then increasing the density of application as confidence grows. Remembering colouring can always be darkened but lightening lines can be difficult!
2. The main focal point with this portrait is the eyes. Pay particular attention to maintaining their soulful expression, as this helps create the particular mood for the piece.
3. The nasal zone has a different texture to it. This should be subtle, yet noticeable. To achieve this, maintain rendering light enough to appreciate the created patterns.
4. The entire head does not need to be drawn to create an impact. Here the composition draws attention to the eyes and their expression. The edges can be left unfinished to give a mere suggestion as to the dogs laying position.

Drawing Dogs

MIXED BREED 2

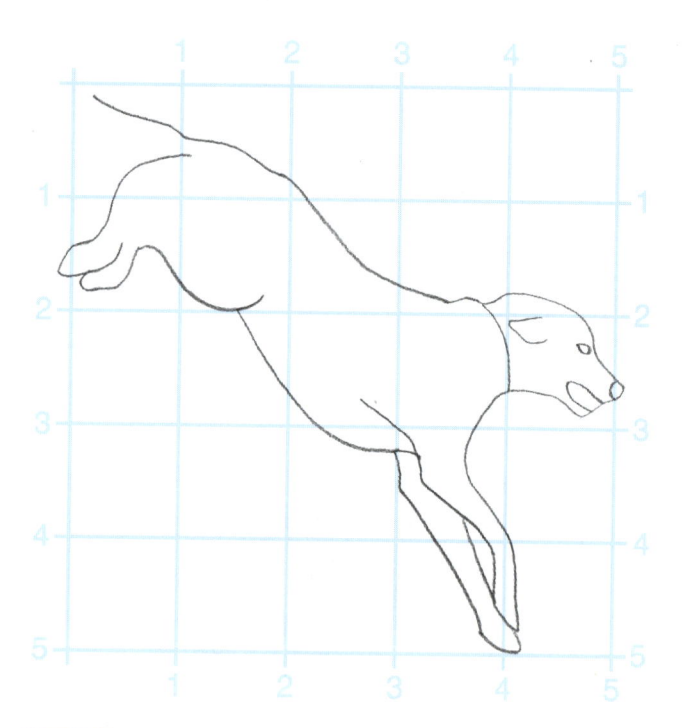

STEP 1:
On your own piece of paper, begin by very lightly drawing a twenty-five square grid using a ruler. A standard 2B pencil is ideal to draw basic circles and lines, as well as the main shapes of the finished sketch. Use the grid to help create accurate proportions.

STEP 2:
Lightly sketching, follow the basic shapes you have just created and develop the outline of the image and its features. Still focusing on proportions and accuracy.

STEP 3:
When satisfied with your outlines, use an eraser to tidy any unnecessary lines or mistakes.

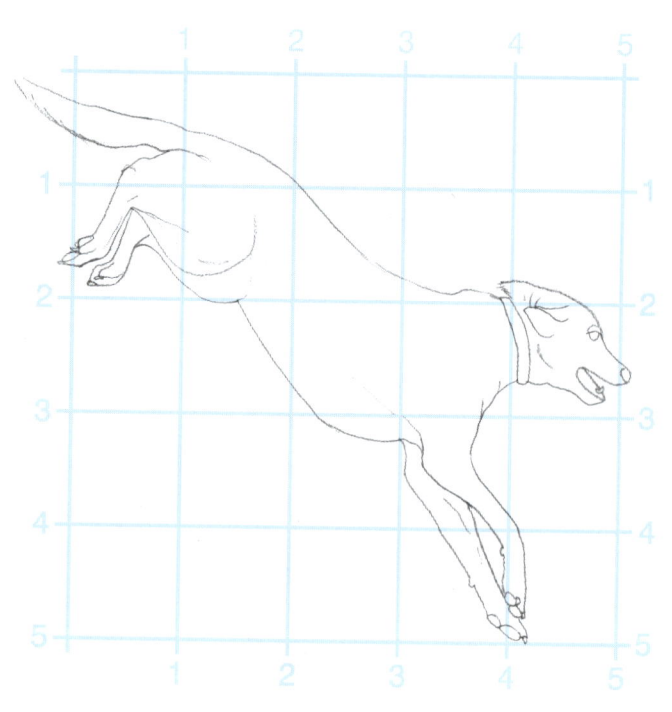

STEP 4:
Using a 4B and a 6B pencil to lightly render the image, copy the techniques shown in the example and read the observation details to help achieve an accurate result.

Drawing Dogs

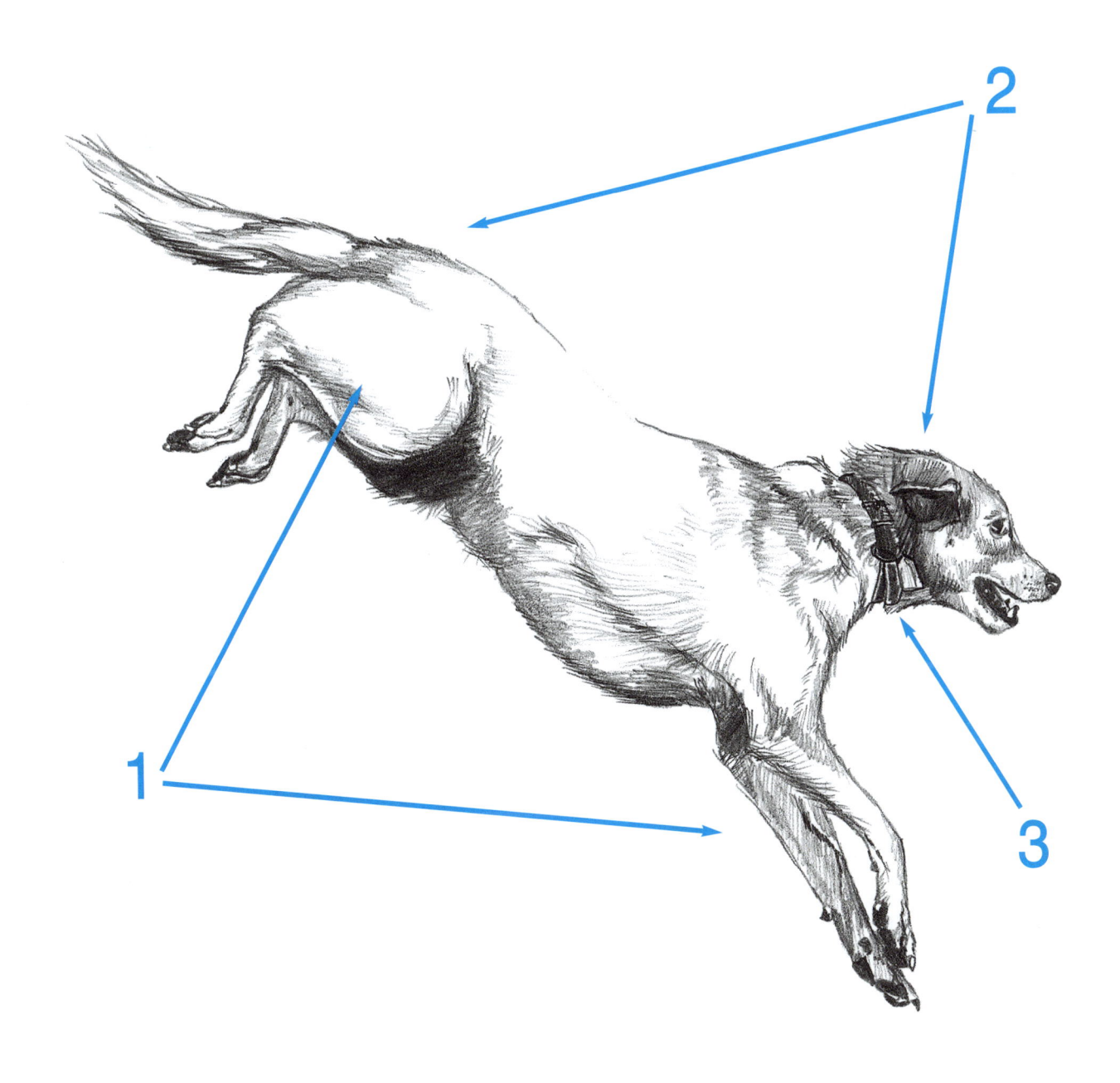

OBSERVATION DETAILS:

1. A dog's body has many powerful muscles, allowing it to effectively run and jump. Notice how the hind legs curl up and the front legs stretch out as it prepares to land. Make sure the angles and positions of the legs are accurately drawn.
2. The position of the dog's head, legs and body mass are at quite an exaggerated angle. This creates the illusion he has jumped over something very large. If this angle is incorrect the dog will seem unbalanced. If uncertain of the correct positioning, use a pencil to make the same angle as the example shown, then keeping that angle, follow it across to your own drawing. This will indicate accuracy and with a few adjustments, this will reveal the greatest proficiency.
3. When drawing a dog portrait, or any portrait for that matter; it is helpful to include personal items such as a dog collar, a favourite toy, or objects significant to that subject. This adds further visual interest to the composition and shows their personality and character.

Drawing Dogs

GOLDEN RETRIEVER

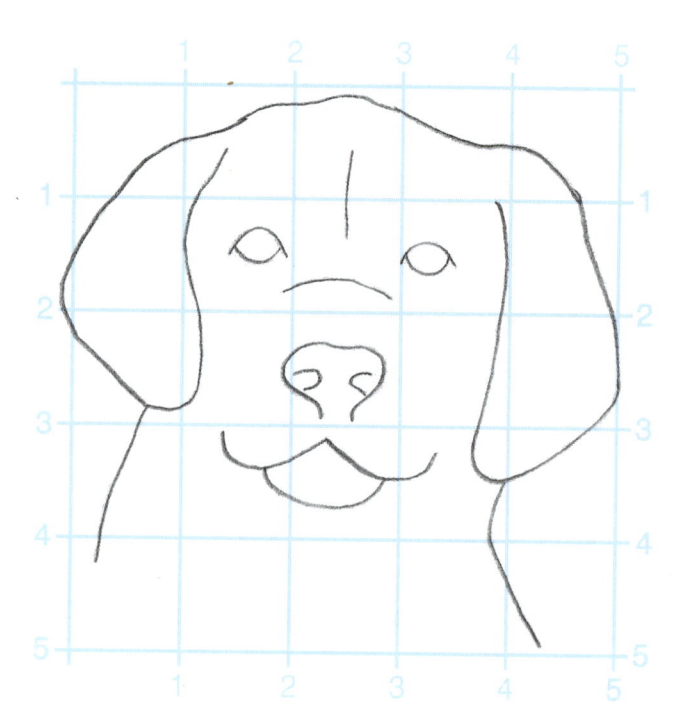

STEP 1:
On your own piece of paper, begin by very lightly drawing a twenty-five square grid using a ruler. A standard 2B pencil is ideal to draw basic circles and lines, as well as the main shapes of the finished sketch. Use the grid to help create accurate proportions.

STEP 2:
Lightly sketching, follow the basic shapes you have just created and develop the outline of the image and its features. Still focusing on proportions and accuracy.

STEP 3:
When satisfied with your outlines, use an eraser to tidy any unnecessary lines or mistakes.

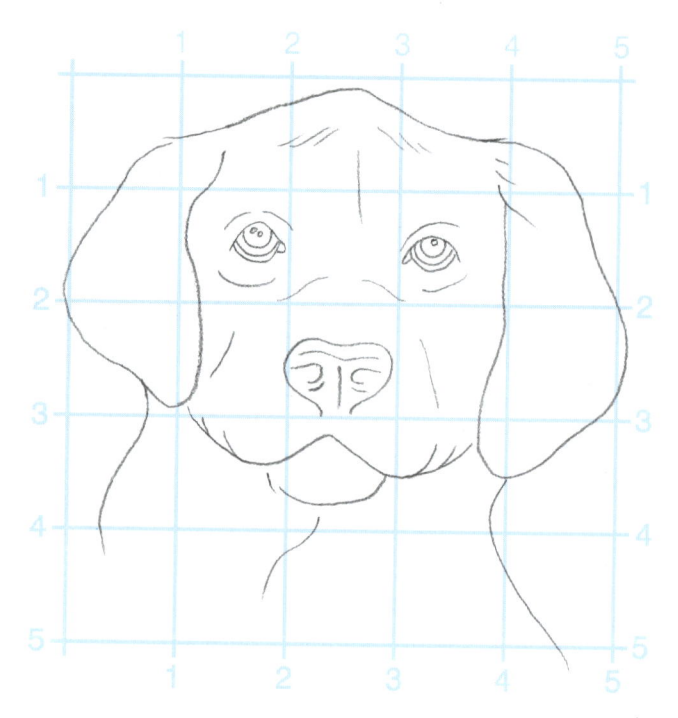

STEP 4:
Using a 4B and a 6B pencil to lightly render the image, copy the techniques shown in the example and read the observation details to help achieve an accurate result.

Drawing Dogs

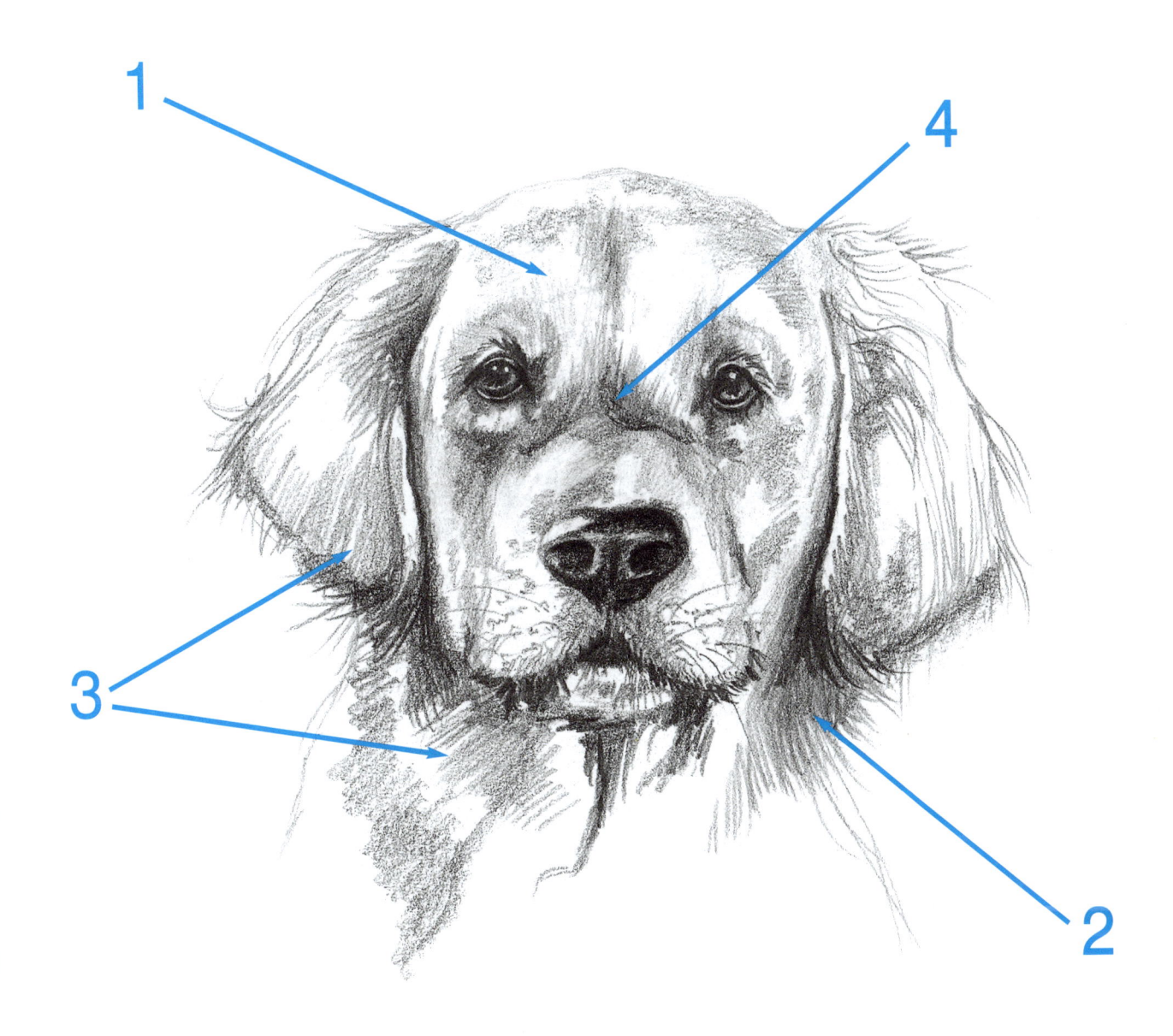

OBSERVATION DETAILS:

1. Start softly, then create density using further strokes. Use this to emphasise specific features. Practise on a separate piece of paper until confident with the application. This will remove the hard edge from shading and make it more consistent.
2. Trying to create realistic long fur on an animal, requires irregular strokes. Otherwise the fur will be seen as too much in the same direction and have less perceived movement.
3. The fur of the Golden Retriever is a light colour, as their name suggests. Be careful when rendering and creating flowing strokes for the hair, ensuring the fur does not appear too dark through excessive strokes.
4. The shadows above the muzzle and eye sockets should be of a medium tone, yet still dark enough to bring the nose forward. This will create a three-dimensional effect, with darker tones under the ears and along the folds of the mouth. Shadows around the nose however should be shaded significantly lighter.

How To Draw Dogs

AFGHAN

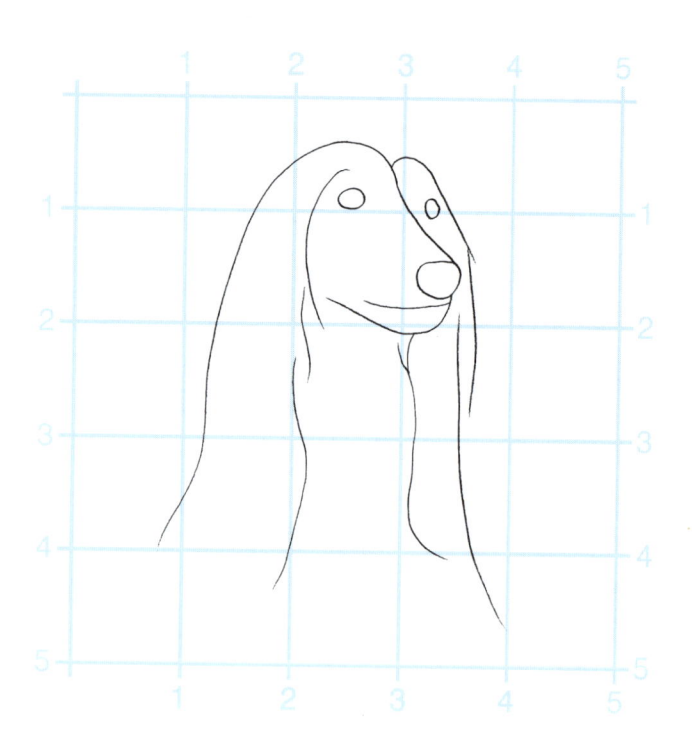

STEP 1:
On your own piece of paper, begin by very lightly drawing a twenty-five square grid using a ruler. A standard 2B pencil is ideal to draw basic circles and lines, as well as the main shapes of the finished sketch. Use the grid to help create accurate proportions.

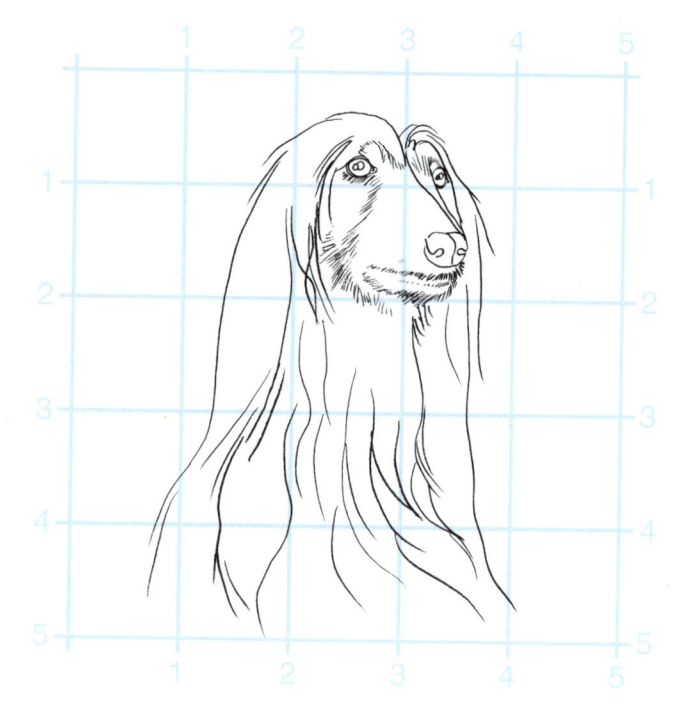

STEP 2:
When satisfied with this outline stage, erase unnecessary lines or mistakes so your illustration is both neat and well-proportioned.

STEP 3:
Using a 4B and a 6B pencil to lightly render the image, copy the techniques shown in the example and read the observation details, to help achieve an accurate result.

Drawing Dogs

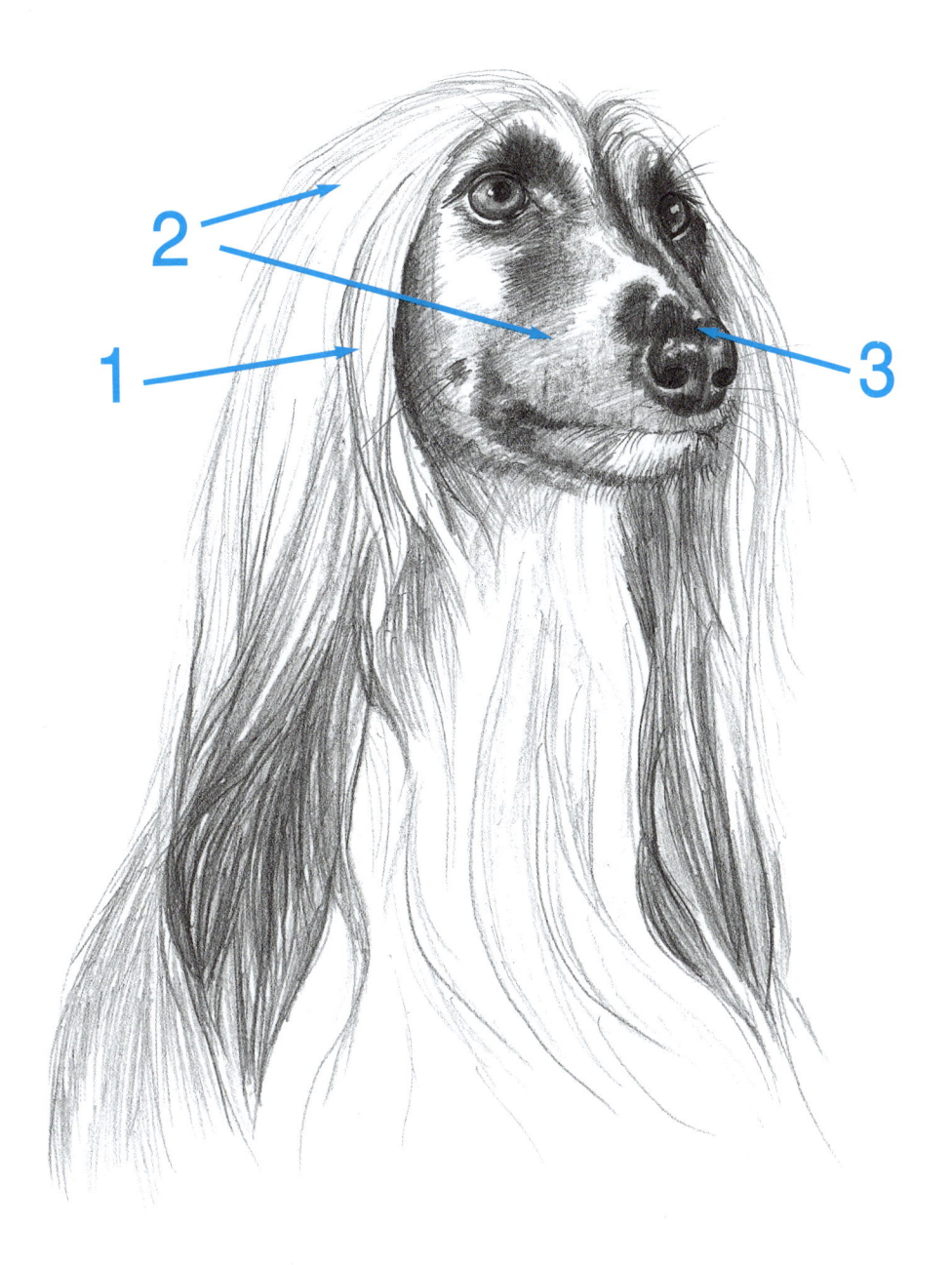

OBSERVATION DETAILS:

1. The Afghan has such long hair, hiding the presence of the accompanying long ears. The darker fur at the base of the ear's hair becomes important, as this is the only defining feature to indicate where the ears end.
2. Rendering fur of different colours when drawing in graphite (black and white) can be a challenge. Each shade must look different to the next. Begin rendering the hair on the top of the head and around the muzzle as one is black and should be the darker. The other is a tan colour, which should appear half as dark. The chest hair, as this is white, requires little rendering.
3. The Afghan's nose or muzzle, is very long, and is characteristic of this breed. In this pose however, the muzzle area appears shortened unlike a side on effect which reveals a long snout. To create the feeling of depth for the protruding muzzle, concentrate on the accuracy of the highlights and shadows.

Drawing Dogs

WEIMARANER

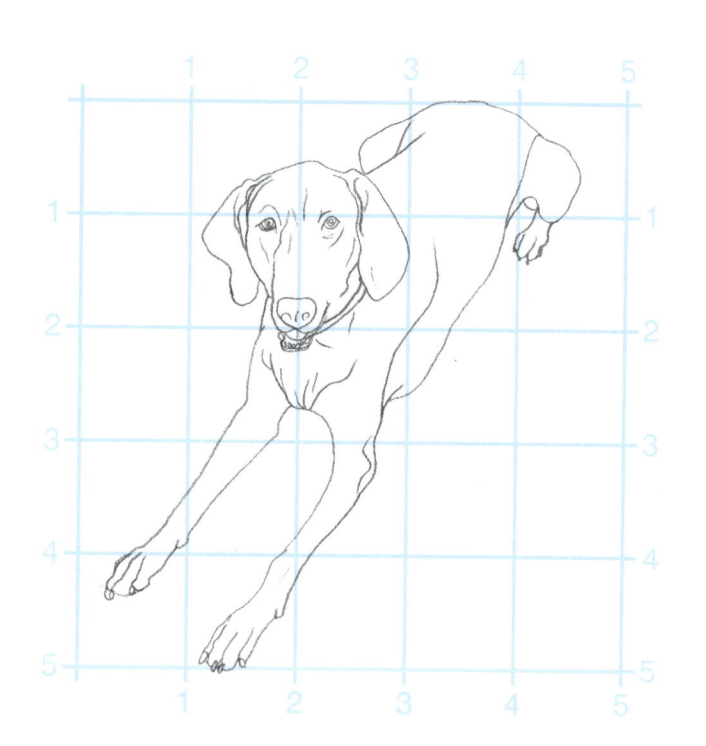

STEP 1:
On your own piece of paper, begin by very lightly drawing a twenty-five square grid using a ruler. A standard 2B pencil is ideal to draw basic circles and lines, as well as the main shapes of the finished sketch. Use the grid to help create accurate proportions.

STEP 2:
When satisfied with this outline stage, erase unnecessary lines or mistakes so your illustration is both neat and well-proportioned.

STEP 3:
Using a 4B and a 6B pencil to lightly render the image, copy the techniques shown in the example and read the observation details to help achieve an accurate result.

Drawing Dogs

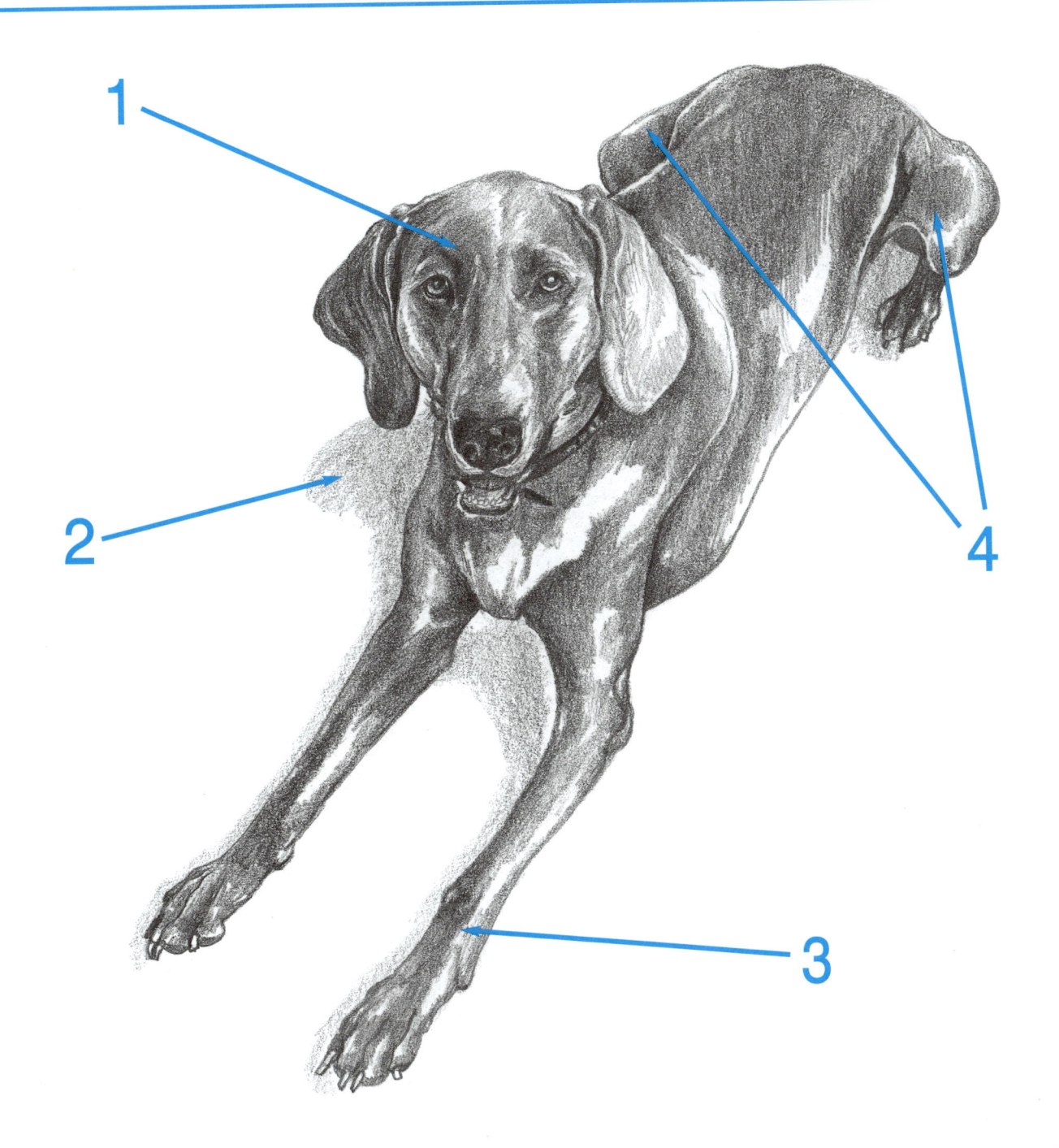

OBSERVATION DETAILS:

1. This dog has short and shiny hair, therefore the feature requires much more shading. Make an effort not to make the strokes too dark, as facial features and other necessary details can be lost.
2. Adding a shadow to the underside of the dog creates a base on which to lay, providing greater realism. Shadows should be drawn to the left, consistent with the light source. If unsure, place the shadows to the opposite side of highlighted features.
3. The front legs and paws will dramatically effect the whole perspective if drawn incorrectly. If alignment is difficult use your pencil to measure the length of the legs, comparing this to another part of the body. This will help achieve correct proportions and angles.
4. When laying down, hind legs are usually tucked underneath the body, revealing only the paws. The shape these hind quarters make is important in showing the muscles and the way the skin stretches when in this position.

Drawing Dogs

AIREDALE TERRIER

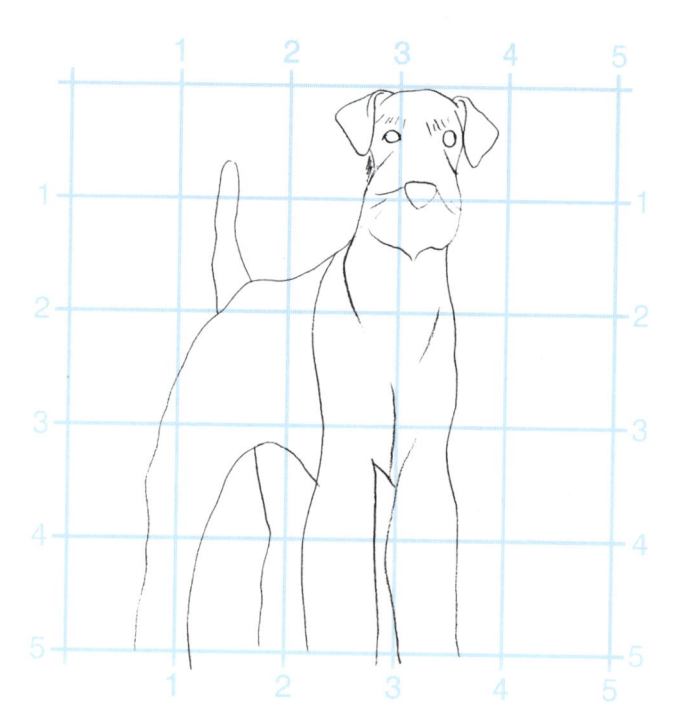

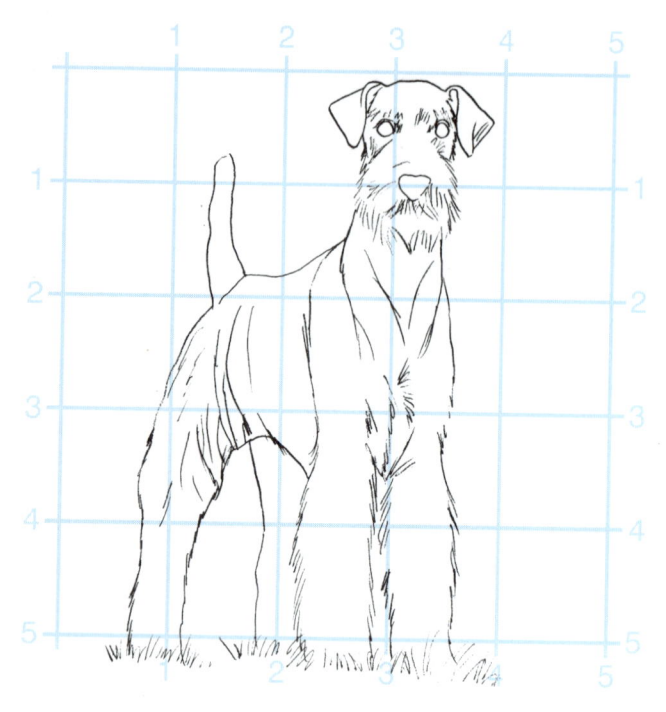

STEP 1:
On your own piece of paper, begin by very lightly drawing a twenty-five square grid using a ruler. A standard 2B pencil is ideal to draw basic circles and lines, as well as the main shapes of the finished sketch. Use the grid to help create accurate proportions.

STEP 2:
When satisfied with this outline stage, erase unnecessary lines or mistakes so your illustration is both neat and well-proportioned.

STEP 3:
Using a 4B and a 6B pencil to lightly render the image, copy the techniques shown in the example and read the observation details to help achieve an accurate result.

Drawing Dogs

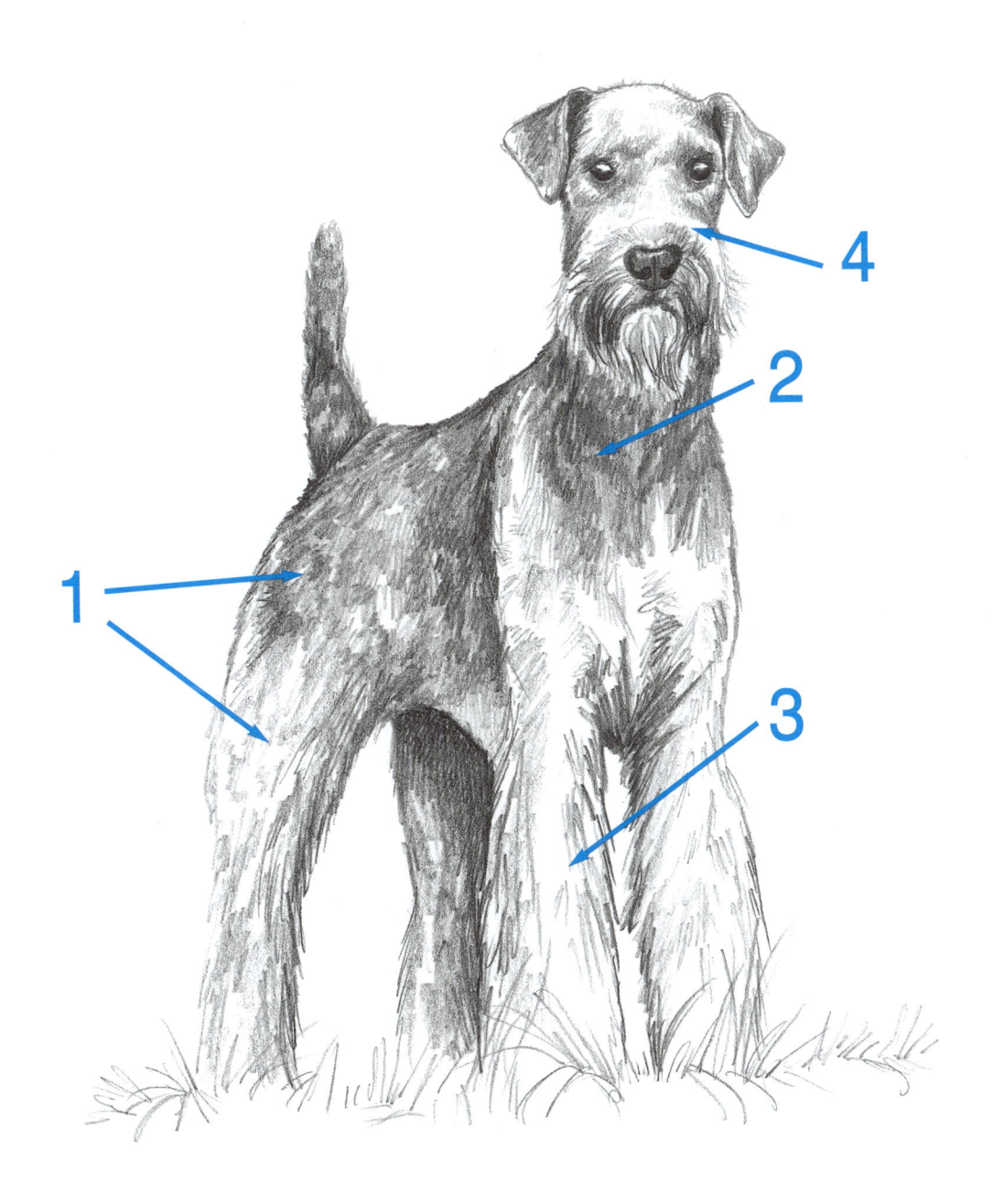

OBSERVATION DETAILS:

1. The Airedale's coat has coarse wavy fur. Create texture by using a sketchy style in these sections which will avoid the appearance of smoother shading.
2. The skin around the chest and neck is loose. Shading here should still be sketchy, but considerably darker.
3. The legs have long hair covering them, hiding their true shape. As this hair is bulky and quite long, shade in the areas of shadow only, avoiding the appearance of a large grey mass.
4. The top of the muzzle needs to be prominent against the rest of the face, giving dimension.

Drawing Dogs

BULLDOG

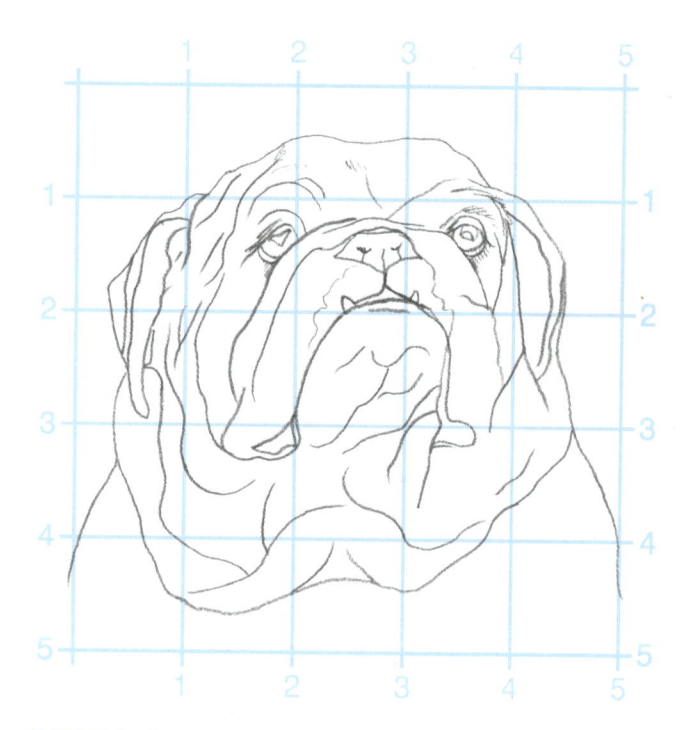

STEP 1:
On your own piece of paper, begin by very lightly drawing a twenty-five square grid using a ruler. A standard 2B pencil is ideal to draw basic circles and lines, as well as the main shapes of the finished sketch. Use the grid to help create accurate proportions.

STEP 2:
When satisfied with this outline stage, erase unnecessary lines or mistakes so your illustration is both neat and well-proportioned.

STEP 3:
Using a 4B and a 6B pencil to lightly render the image, copy the techniques shown in the example and read the observation details to help achieve an accurate result.

Drawing Dogs

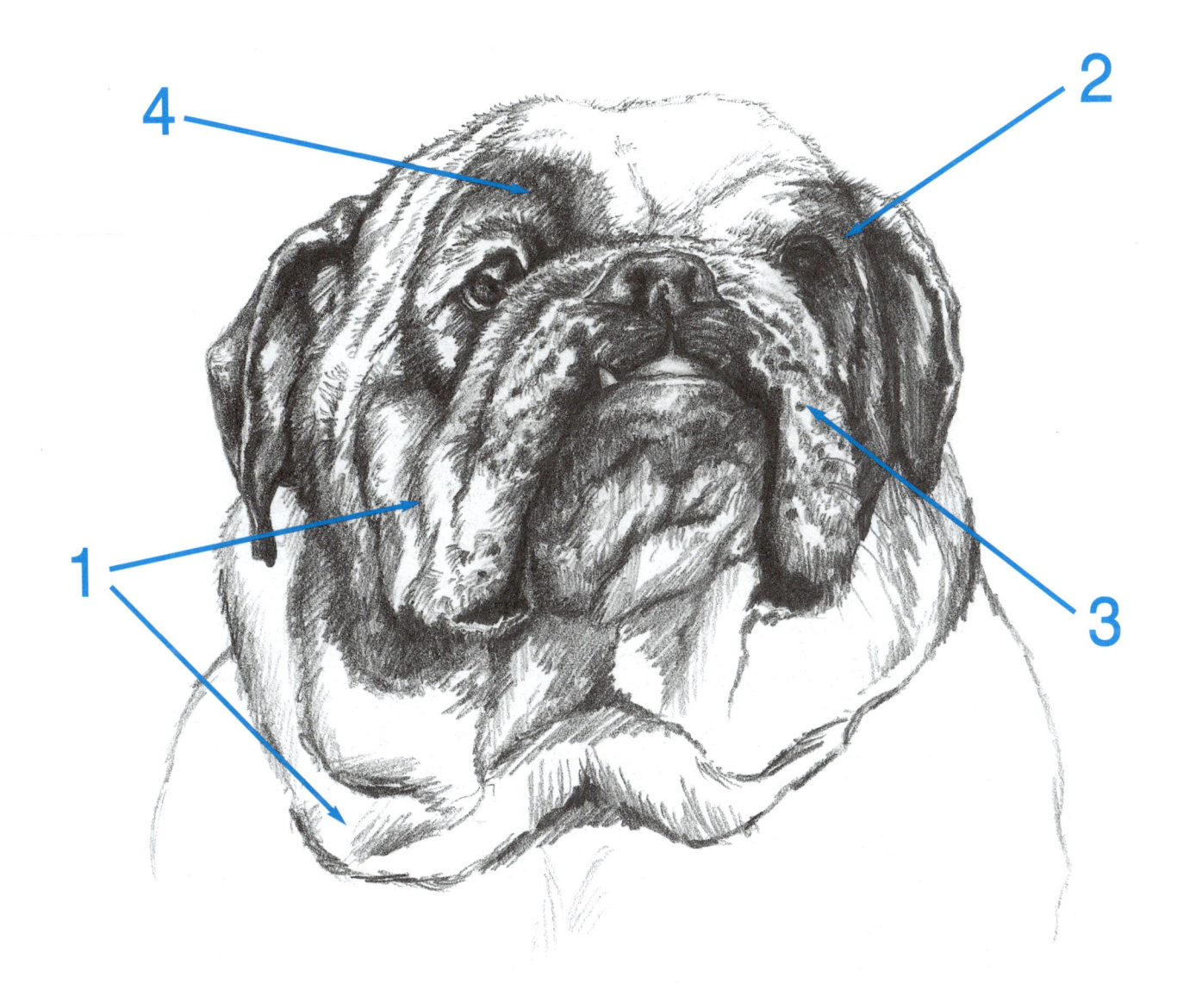

OBSERVATION DETAILS:

1. Characteristically the bulldog has very loose skin and appears "floppy" around the face and chest. This must be recreated accurately as it is a strong feature, revealing his personality and recognisable facial characteristics.

2. The second eye falls behind shadow, however there should still be definition to it. Try not to lose any details by shading too strongly over the top. Draw the basic shapes to begin with, then shade to acknowledge markings and lighting.

3. The Bulldog has a significant number of pronounced dimples where the whiskers belong. As his skin is droopy, these spots can be drawn roughly and should form vague lines when getting closer to the nose region, although spaced further down the jowls.

4. As with the Pug, focus on the dark patches around the eyes, use them to enhance the facial features. They can become tools of expression, as the eyebrows do on a human, with the shape raised slightly at the peak and slightly exaggerated.

Drawing Dogs

BULL TERRIER

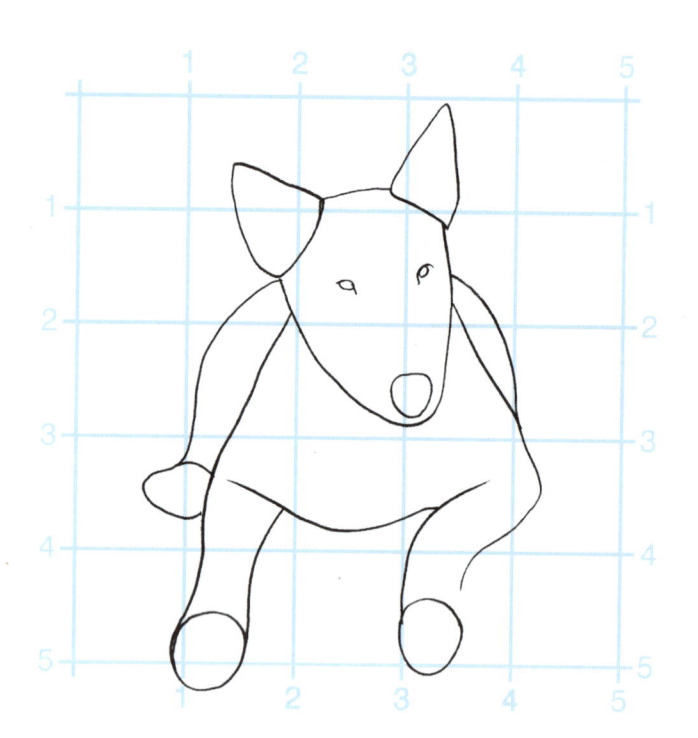

STEP 1:
On your own piece of paper, begin by very lightly drawing a twenty-five square grid using a ruler. A standard 2B pencil is ideal to draw basic circles and lines, as well as the main shapes of the finished sketch. Use the grid to help create accurate proportions.

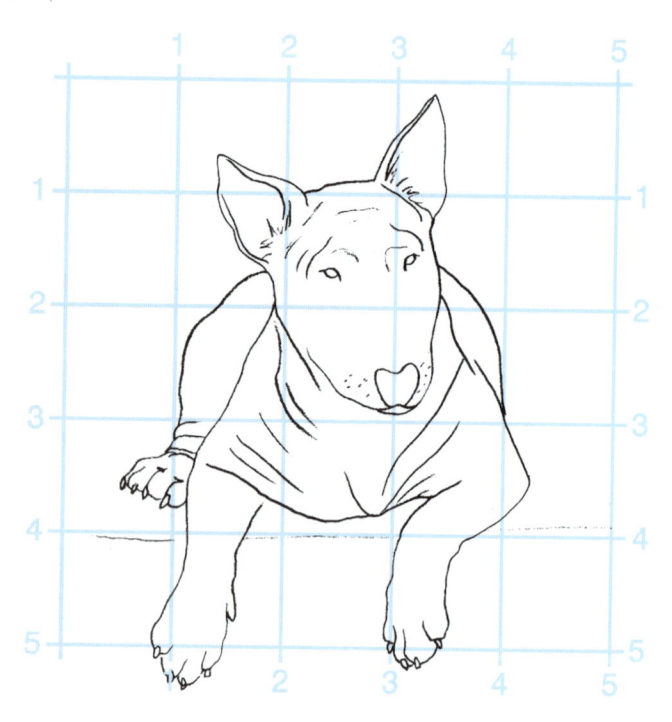

STEP 2:
When satisfied with this outline stage, erase unnecessary lines or mistakes so your illustration is both neat and well-proportioned.

STEP 3:
Using a 4B and a 6B pencil to lightly render the image, copy the techniques shown in the example and read the observation details to help achieve an accurate result.

Drawing Dogs

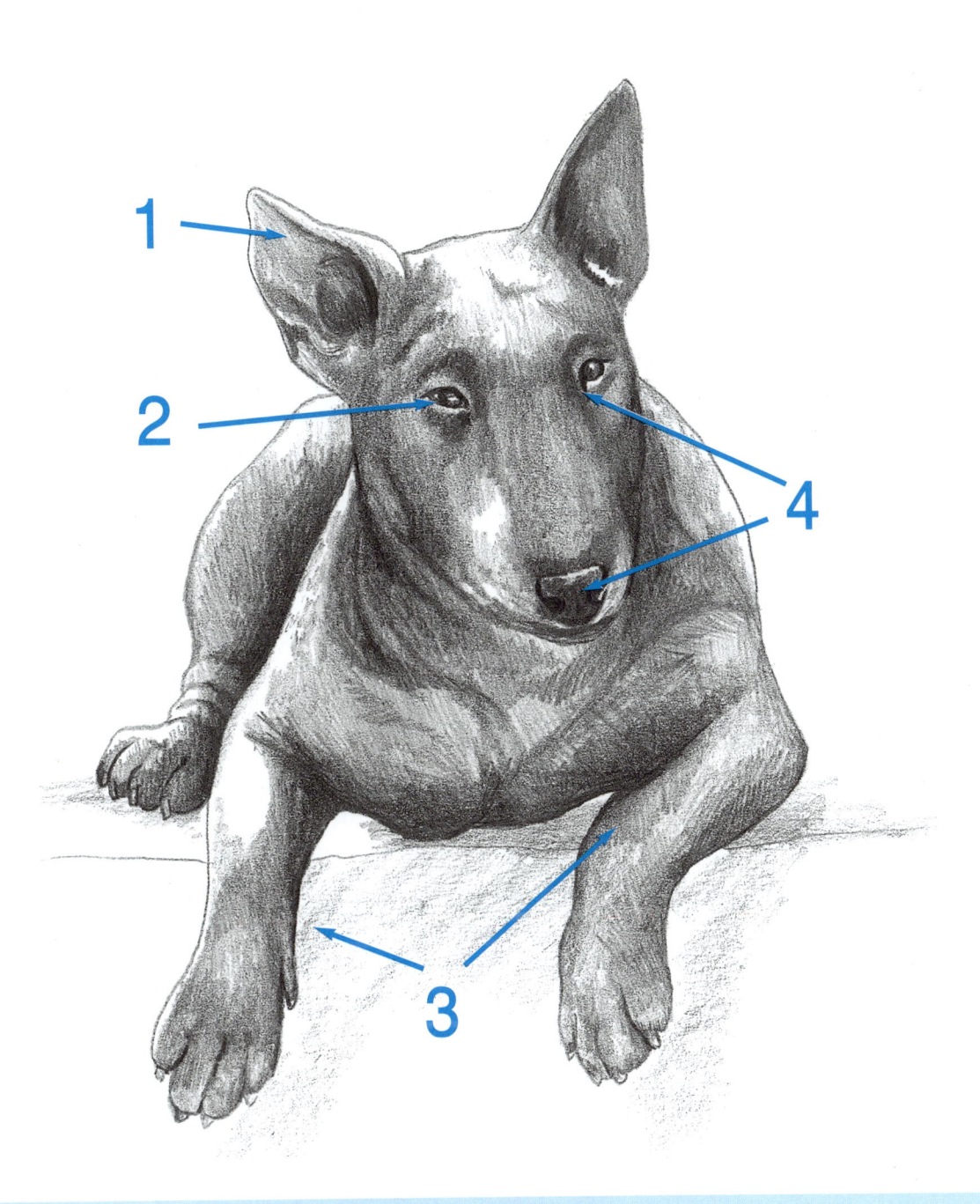

OBSERVATION DETAILS:

1. The Bull Terrier has quite large pointy ears. When detailing these it is most important that the correct proportion to the head is maintained.
2. The eyes appear small and squinty and you may find it difficult giving them expression. Use the eyebrows and surrounding areas of the eyes to show the strength of character.
3. This composition has legs and paws dangling over a ledge, giving the viewer another perspective. Relaxed poses can often be more interesting than standing or sitting. It may also be more challenging when drawing some limbs whilst others are hidden from view. In these instances both muscles and body shape will change accordingly.
4. The darkest parts of this illustration should be the eyes and nose. Avoid rendering the rest of the body too heavily.

Drawing Dogs

DACHSHUND

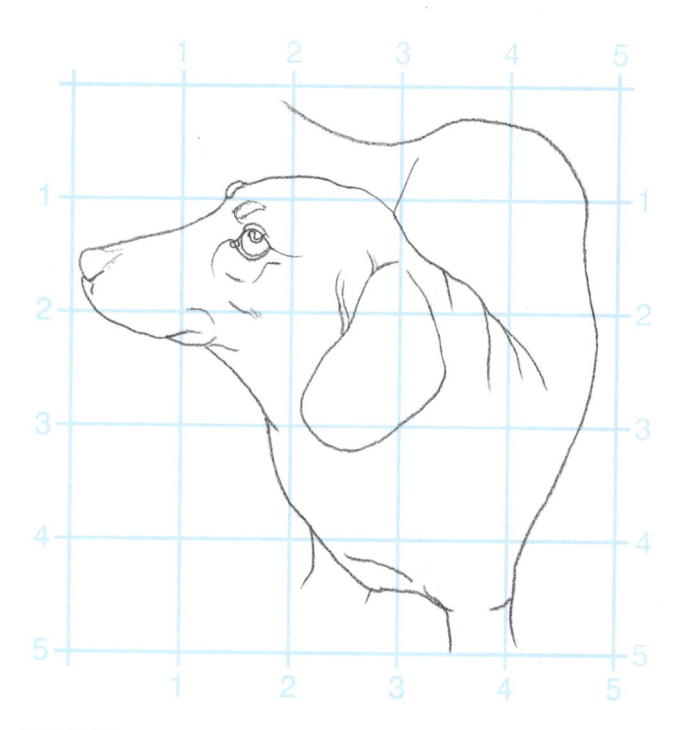

STEP 1:
On your own piece of paper, begin by very lightly drawing a twenty-five square grid using a ruler. A standard 2B pencil is ideal to draw basic circles and lines, as well as the main shapes of the finished sketch. Use the grid to help create accurate proportions.

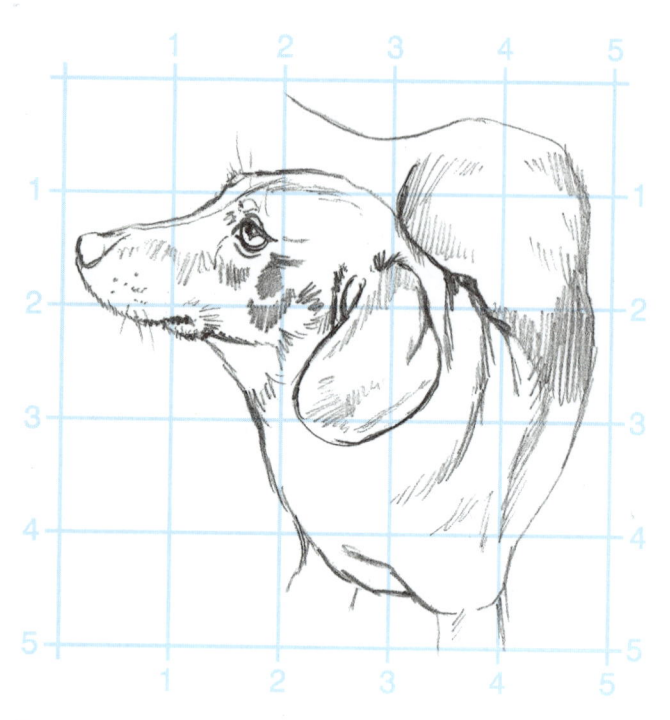

STEP 2:
When satisfied with this outline stage, erase unnecessary lines or mistakes so your illustration is both neat and well-proportioned.

STEP 3:
Using a 4B and a 6B pencil to lightly render the image, copy the techniques shown in the example and read the observation details to help achieve an accurate result.

Drawing Dogs

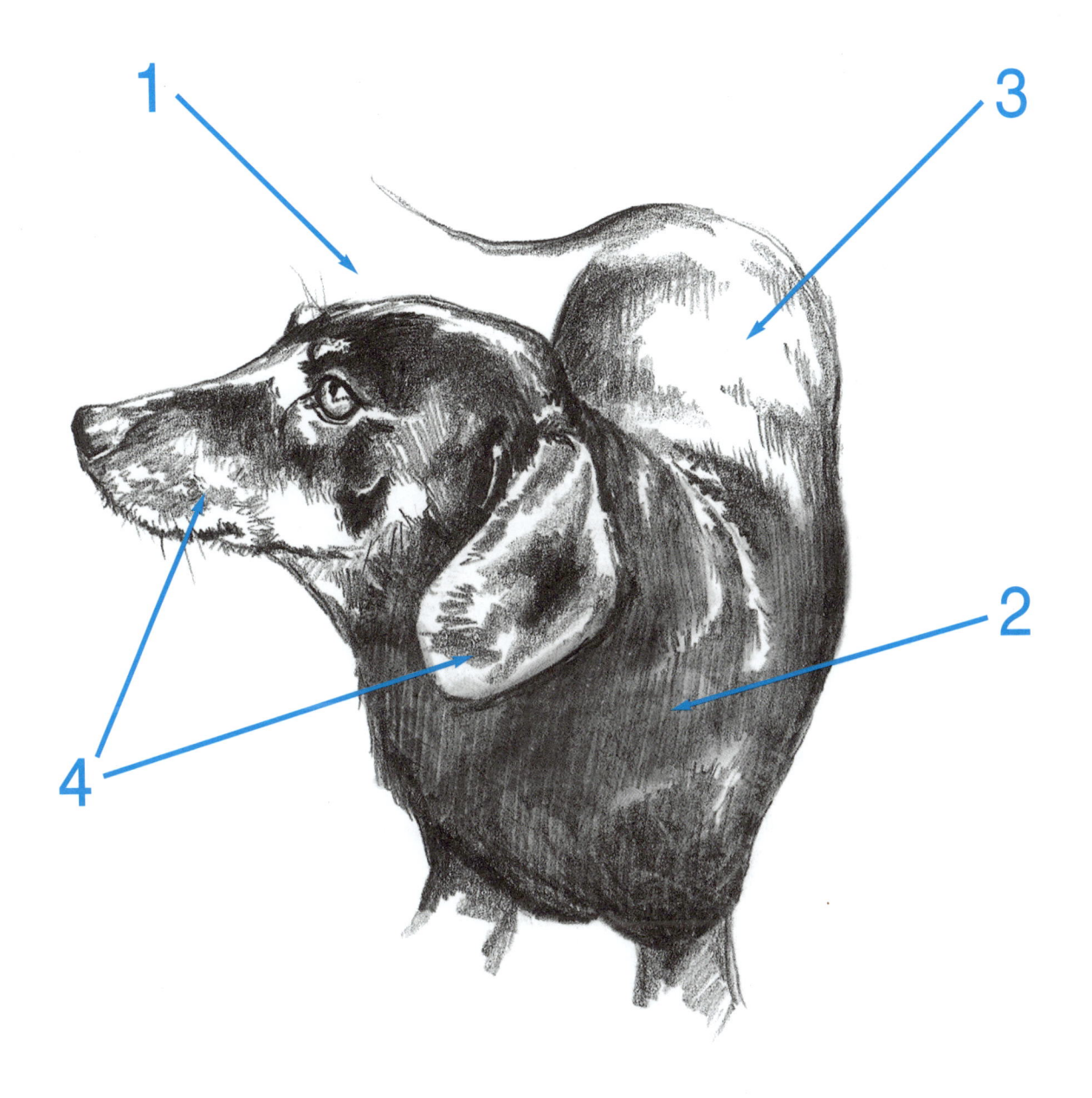

OBSERVATION DETAILS:

1. This composition is particularly appealing because it leaves only a suggestion as to the body shape. Yet it captures the main characteristics such as the short, long body and tiny legs. The tail is a tapered line giving the viewer the idea as to positioning only. Drawing a single sketched line also enhances the feeling of movement as the tail wags.
2. The fur of the Dachshund is relatively dark and will require the use of a 6B pencil, achieving a smooth and even shading.
3. The reflections and shiny nature of the coat should be shown by leaving white within the shading. This then creates a stark contrast. 6B pencils are very soft and therefore preferred, although care must be taken with rendering. To avoid any smudging, use a clean piece of paper over artwork, on which you rest your hand.
4. The Dachshund has a very long muzzle and rounded ears. Proper results will not be achieved if these features are an incorrect length.

Drawing Dogs
PEKINGESE

STEP 1:
On your own piece of paper, begin by very lightly drawing a twenty-five square grid using a ruler. A standard 2B pencil is ideal to draw basic circles and lines, as well as the main shapes of the finished sketch. Use the grid to help create accurate proportions.

STEP 2:
When satisfied with this outline stage, erase unnecessary lines or mistakes so your illustration is both neat and well-proportioned.

STEP 3:
Using a 4B and a 6B pencil to lightly render the image, copy the techniques shown in the example and read the observation details to help achieve an accurate result.

Drawing Dogs

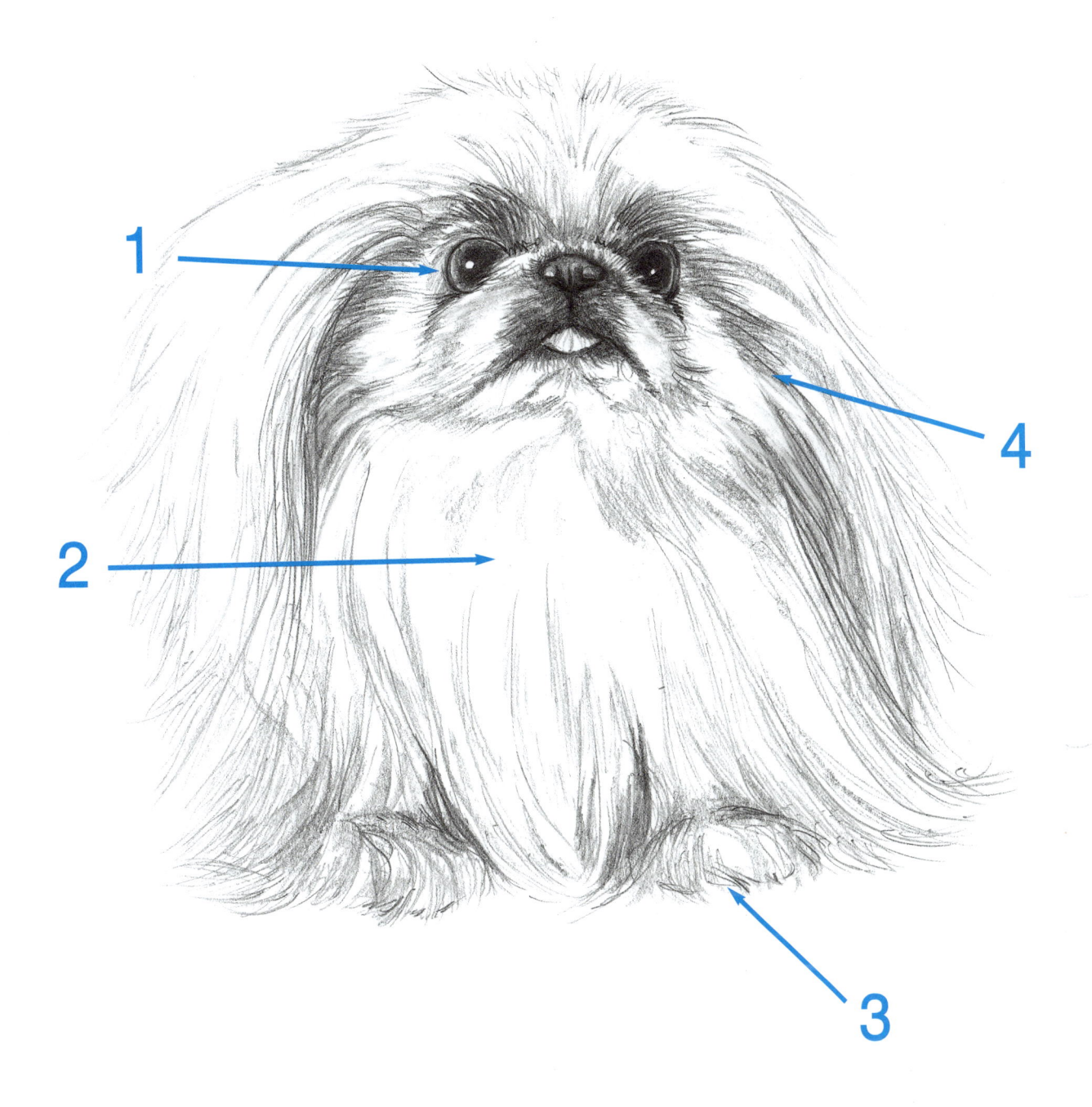

OBSERVATION DETAILS:
1. The Pekingese is a funny little character and great attention needs to be taken to correctly show the facial features, in particular the eyes, being the main focal point.
2. The bulk of the Pekingese's fur should be left white with the only rendering shown to areas of shadow revealing the direction of the flowing hair.
3. The paws are tucked underneath the hair and should not be drawn too conspicuously. They should blend in, particularly as they are heavily haired as well. However they need to appear separate from the chest area. This can be achieved through pencil strokes, making certain the direction of your shading is executed in a curved motion revealing the roundness of the paws
4. Similar to the Afghan Hound, the Pekingese's ears are barely noticeable amongst the bulk of the head and body hair. The shadows will also become important in showing the length and presence of the ears.

Drawing Dogs

SILKY TERRIER

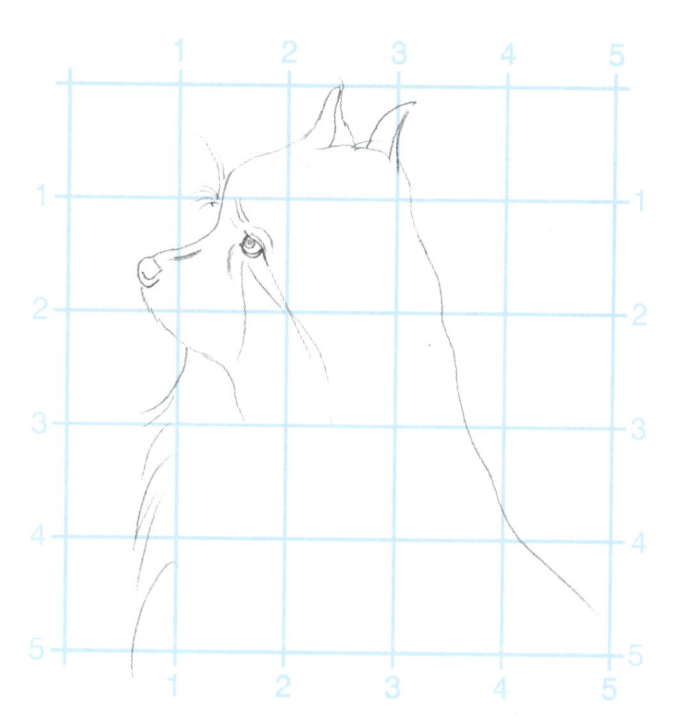

STEP 1:
On your own piece of paper, begin by very lightly drawing a twenty-five square grid using a ruler. A standard 2B pencil is ideal to draw basic circles and lines, as well as the main shapes of the finished sketch. Use the grid to help create accurate proportions.

STEP 2:
When satisfied with this outline stage, erase unnecessary lines or mistakes so your illustration is both neat and well-proportioned.

STEP 3:
Using a 4B and a 6B pencil to lightly render the image, copy the techniques shown in the example and read the observation details to help achieve an accurate result.

Drawing Dogs

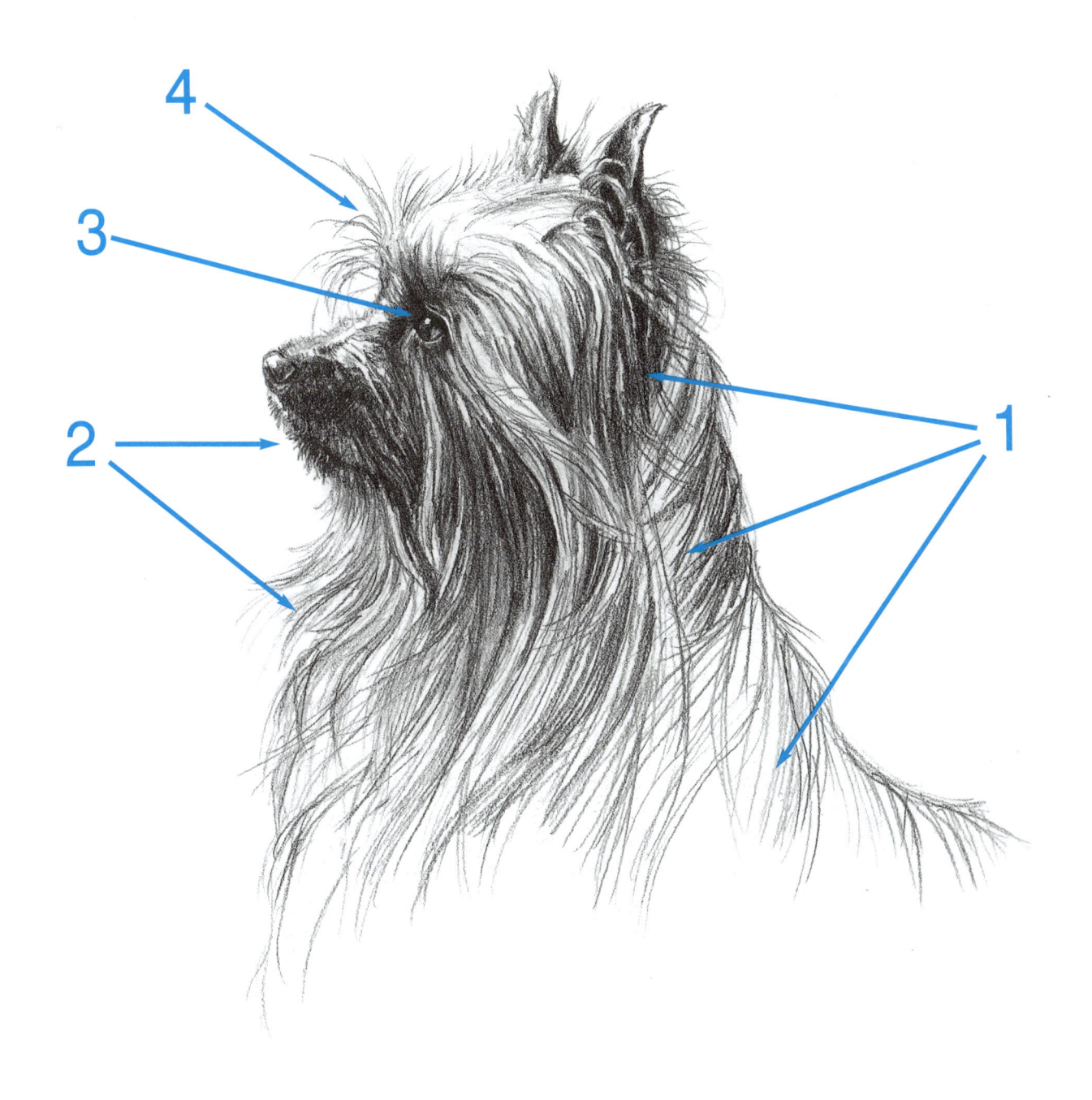

OBSERVATION DETAILS:

1. The hair patterns need not be overly shaded. Over shading will leave the hair looking dull and heavy rather than lively and wispy. Identify the areas of shadow and light, as well as the direction in which the hair flows, only drawing the most significant strands.
2. Keep all the whiskers on the muzzle very delicate and soft. Using light flicks of a sharpened 2B pencil, otherwise the strokes will be too thick. The main aim, to keep the strokes softer and tapering at the tips.
3. Reflection of light on the eyes is very important. Without this, the eyes become lost in shadows and appear dull and lifeless. Before shading the eye, draw the shape of the reflection, then shade the surround.
4. The hair overhanging and strands above the brow, draws the viewers attention to the eye. These hairs should be featured accurately and with a sharp pencil.

Drawing Dogs

SIBERIAN HUSKY

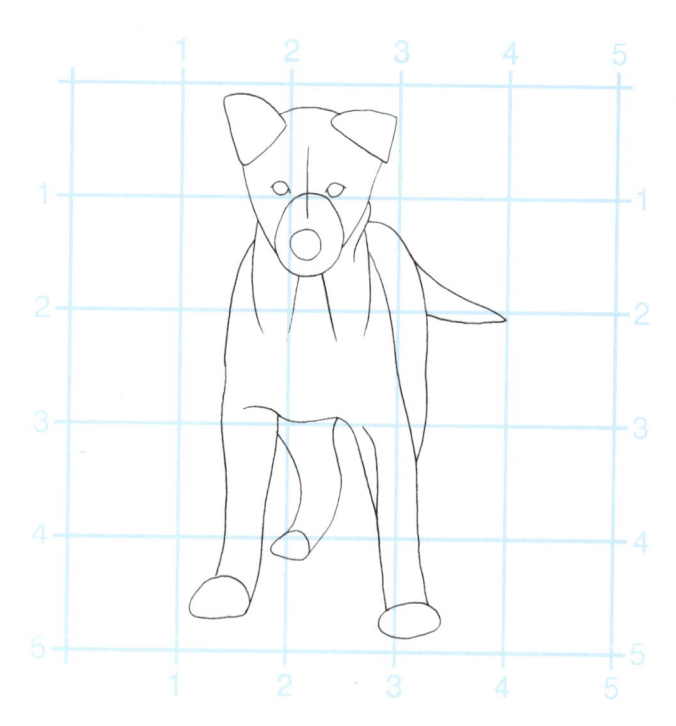

STEP 1:
On your own piece of paper, begin by very lightly drawing a twenty-five square grid using a ruler. A standard 2B pencil is ideal to draw basic circles and lines, as well as the main shapes of the finished sketch. Use the grid to help create accurate proportions.

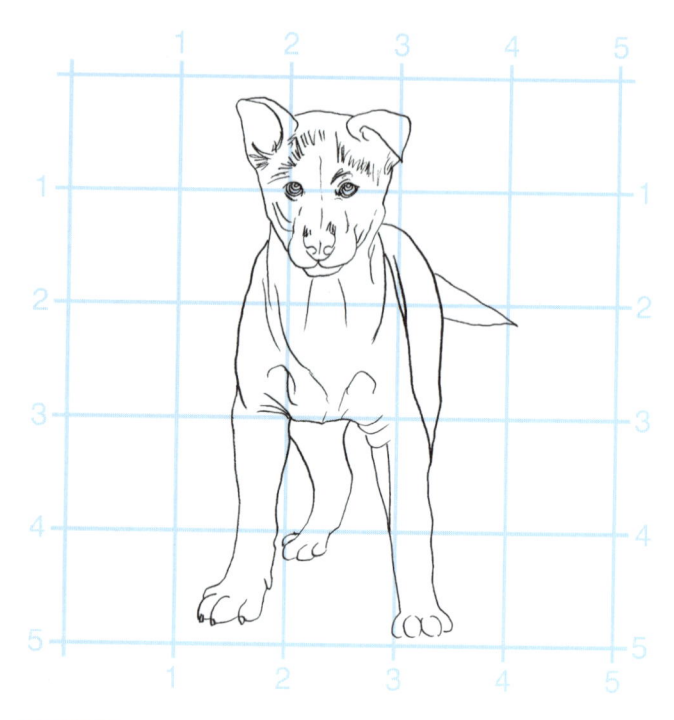

STEP 2:
When satisfied with this outline stage, erase unnecessary lines or mistakes so your illustration is both neat and well-proportioned.

STEP 3:
Using a 4B and a 6B pencil to lightly render the image, copy the techniques shown in the example and read the observation details to help achieve an accurate result.

Drawing Dogs

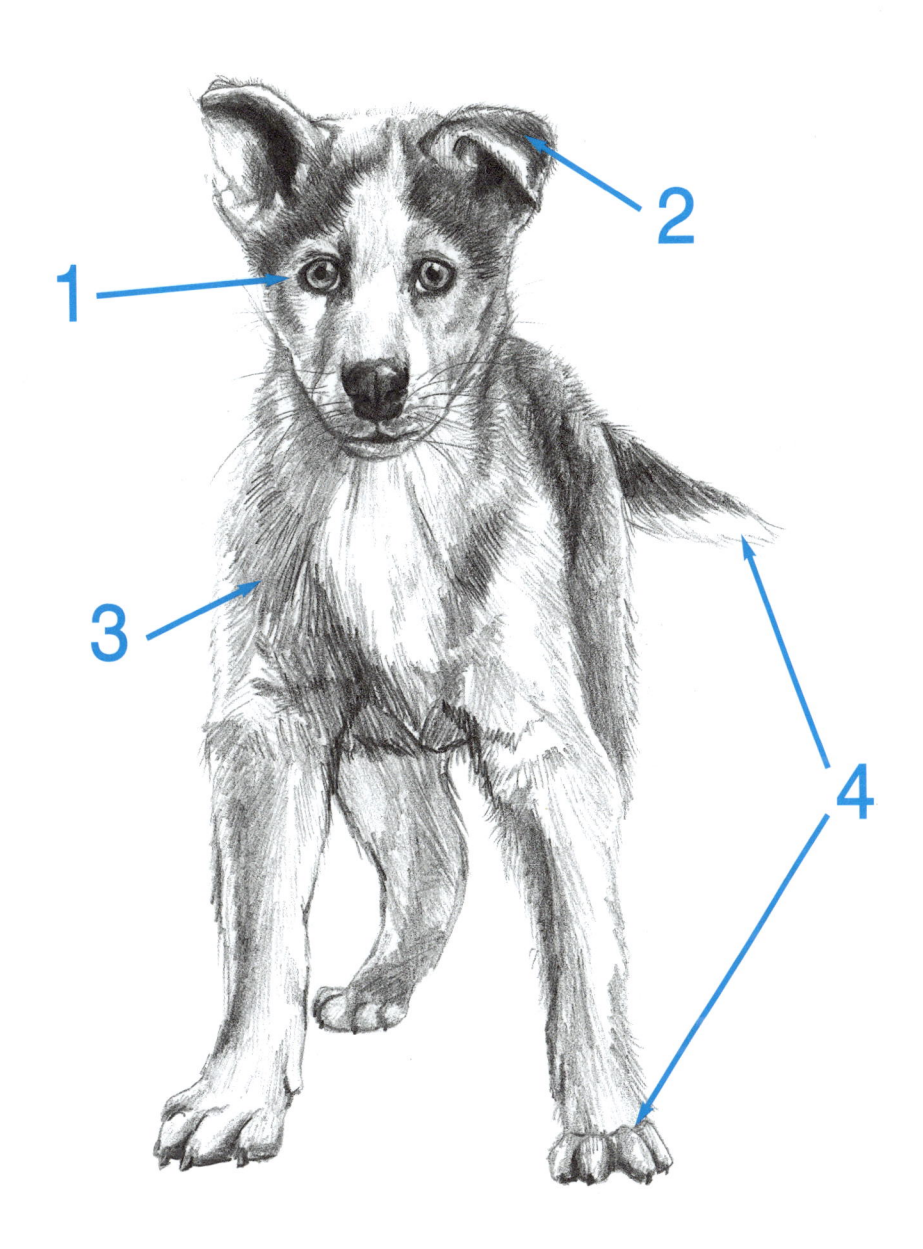

OBSERVATION DETAILS:

1. The eyes of the Husky are particularly important characteristics of this breed. Draw with great care, as they are the focal point of the piece, and the viewer should be drawn to them. The centre of the eye is darkest with the outer surface needing almost no shading at all. Reflections need to remain white and create the illusion of wetness.
2. As this dog is a puppy, the ears have not yet developed with full strength. Note how one ear bends forward with the other straight. Neither are yet pointed as with a mature Siberian Husky.
3. The coat is thick and straight and should be roughly drawn, yet with pencil strokes flowing in the one direction for the hair.
4. Dog paws are quite often seen at an angle as shown in this illustration. Training your eye to notice these differences is valuable, in not only main parts of the body but also smaller aspects such as; ears, tail, paws, nose. These will greatly influence realism and overall success of the representation.

Drawing Dogs

LABRADOR PUPPY

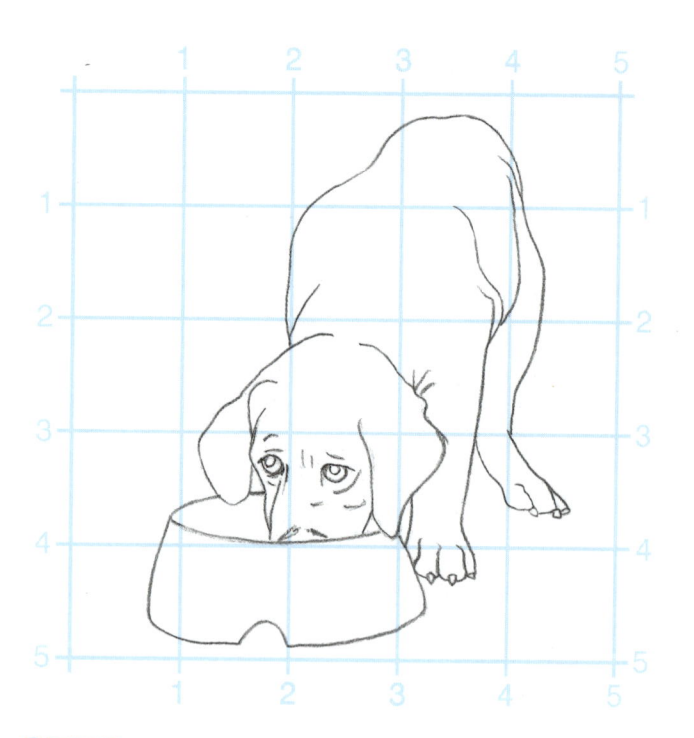

STEP 1:
On your own piece of paper, begin by very lightly drawing a twenty-five square grid using a ruler. A standard 2B pencil is ideal to draw basic circles and lines, as well as the main shapes of the finished sketch. Use the grid to help create accurate proportions.

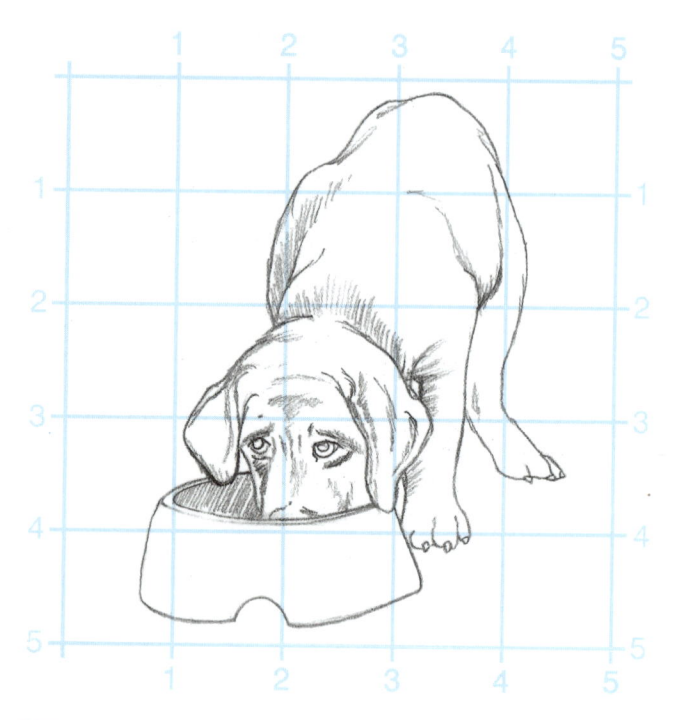

STEP 2:
When satisfied with this outline stage, erase unnecessary lines or mistakes so your illustration is both neat and well-proportioned.

STEP 3:
Using a 4B and a 6B pencil to lightly render the image, copy the techniques shown in the example and read the observation details to help achieve an accurate result.

Drawing Dogs

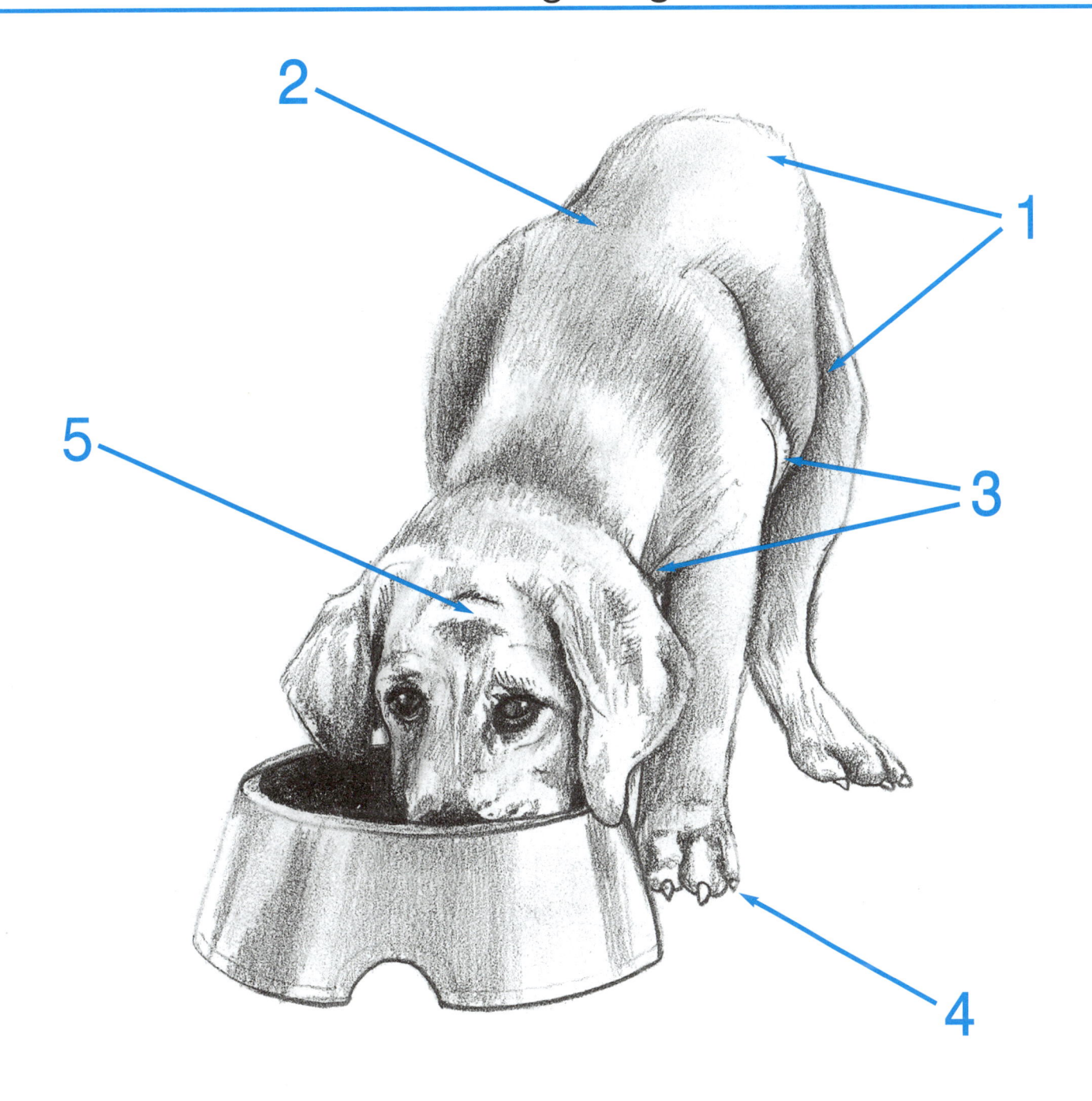

OBSERVATION DETAILS:
1. Distinguishing between areas of shadow and central outlines requires different levels of thickness for the darker or lighter lines of the body.
2. As discussed earlier, using the side of your pencil to capture the softness of the puppy's fur is a sure way to avoid using hard strokes.
3. Drawing the sides of the body, you will notice the skin collects around the legs and neck. This is important when expressing that cuddly, "puppy feel".
4. There are many bones in the paws of a dog. Study how paws rest on the ground, as each angle is very important, giving the impression of weight being placed on the front of the body.
5. The line above the brow should be slightly accentuated, aiding the dog's expression of inquisitiveness, whilst he fixes his thoughts on an activity immediately in front.

Drawing Dogs

WEST HIGHLAND WHITE

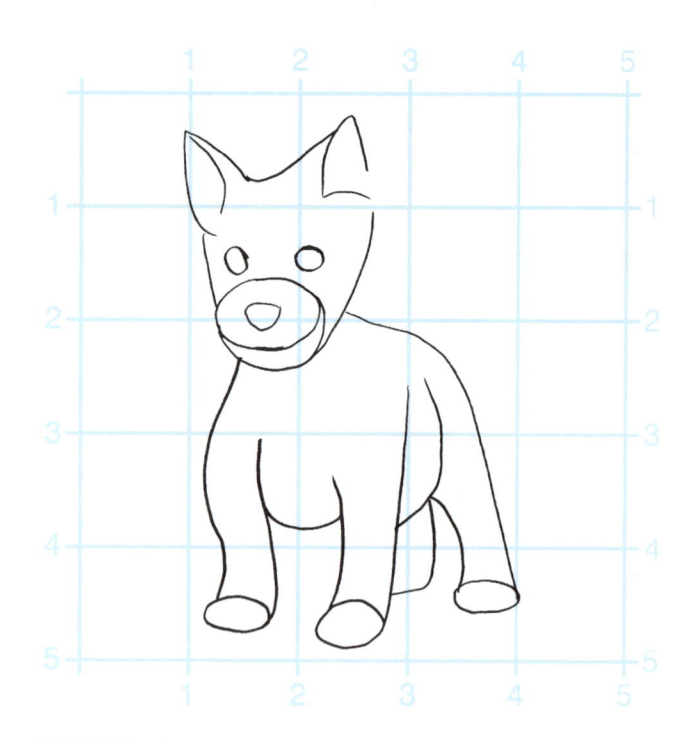

STEP 1:
On your own piece of paper, begin by very lightly drawing a twenty-five square grid using a ruler. A standard 2B pencil is ideal to draw basic circles and lines, as well as the main shapes of the finished sketch. Use the grid to help create accurate proportions.

STEP 2:
When satisfied with this outline stage, erase unnecessary lines or mistakes so your illustration is both neat and well-proportioned.

STEP 3:
Using a 4B and a 6B pencil to lightly render the image, copy the techniques shown in the example and read the observation details to help achieve an accurate result.

Drawing Dogs

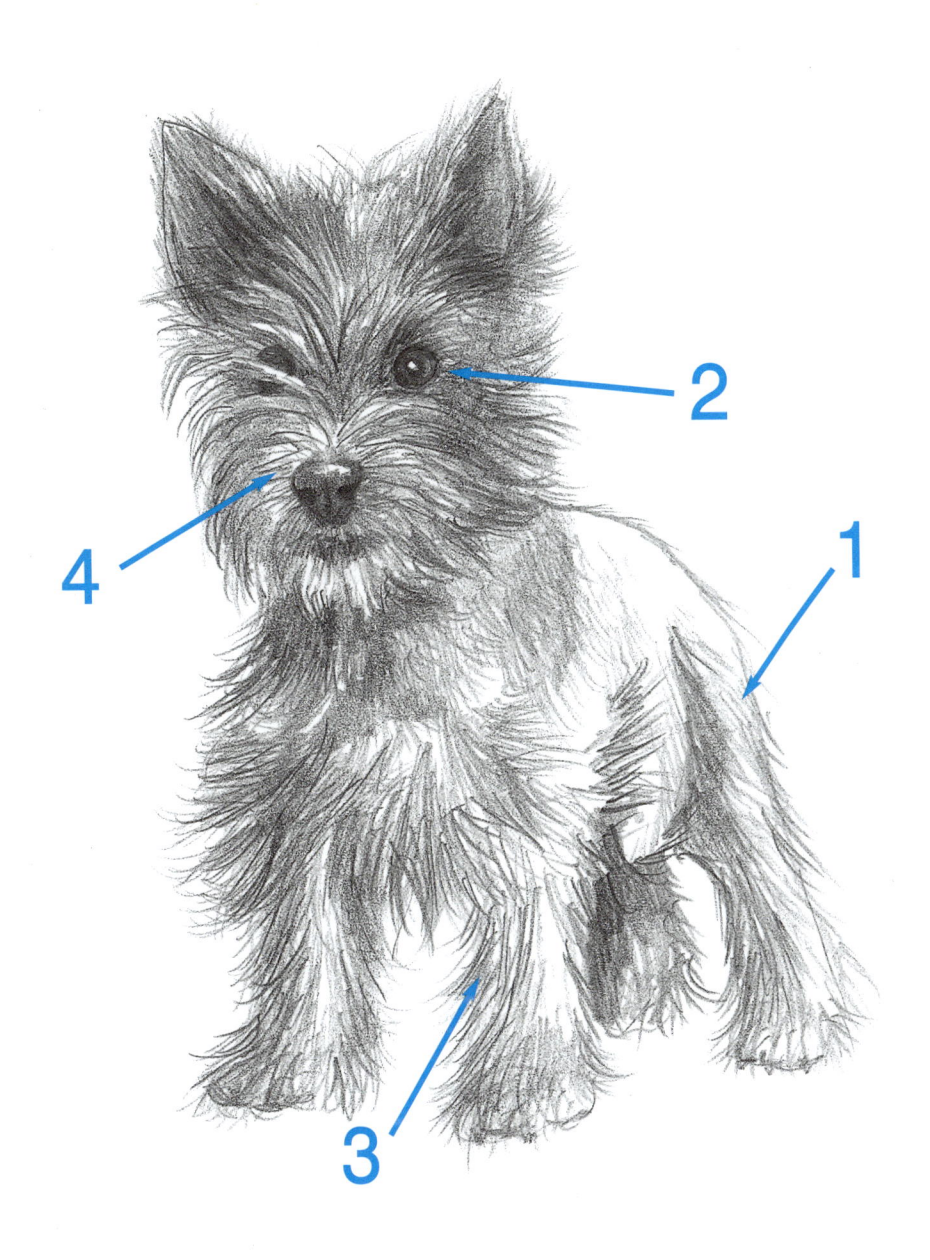

OBSERVATION DETAILS:

1. The Westie in this illustration is a puppy. His hair is not as yet very long and his shape is less bulky than a fully grown dog.
2. The eyes are important in creating the expression on his face. The fur is dense and surrounds the eyes, therefore the eyes should be initially drawn. The white reflection of light in the eyeball is vital in giving the eye character and life.
3. Use a sharpened pencil to illustrate the fur, especially the ends which require a flicking motion, illustrating wispy fur.
4. The hair around the nose needs to be lighter than the rest of the head, bringing it slightly forward. If shading is too heavy, use an eraser to lightly lift small strands of hair, making them appear near white again.

Drawing Dogs

BLACK & TAN COONHOUND

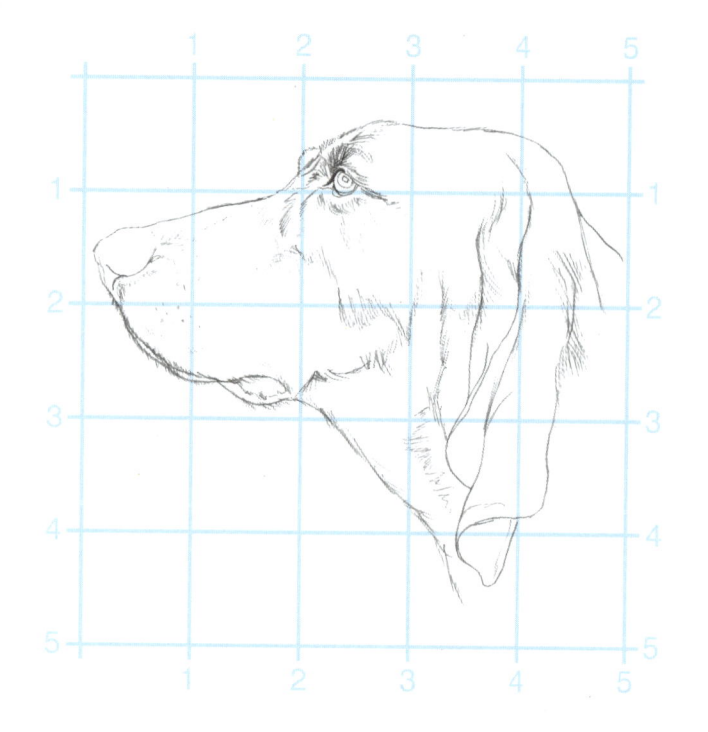

STEP 1:
Use a 2B pencil to draw the outline and details of the dog. Follow the example by creating the main features, as depicted within the finished sketch. When this stage is reached you may need to erase any unnecessary lines or mistakes.

STEP 2:
Using a 4B and a 6B pencil to lightly render the image, copy the techniques shown in the example and read the observation details to help achieve an accurate result.

Drawing Dogs

OBSERVATION DETAILS:

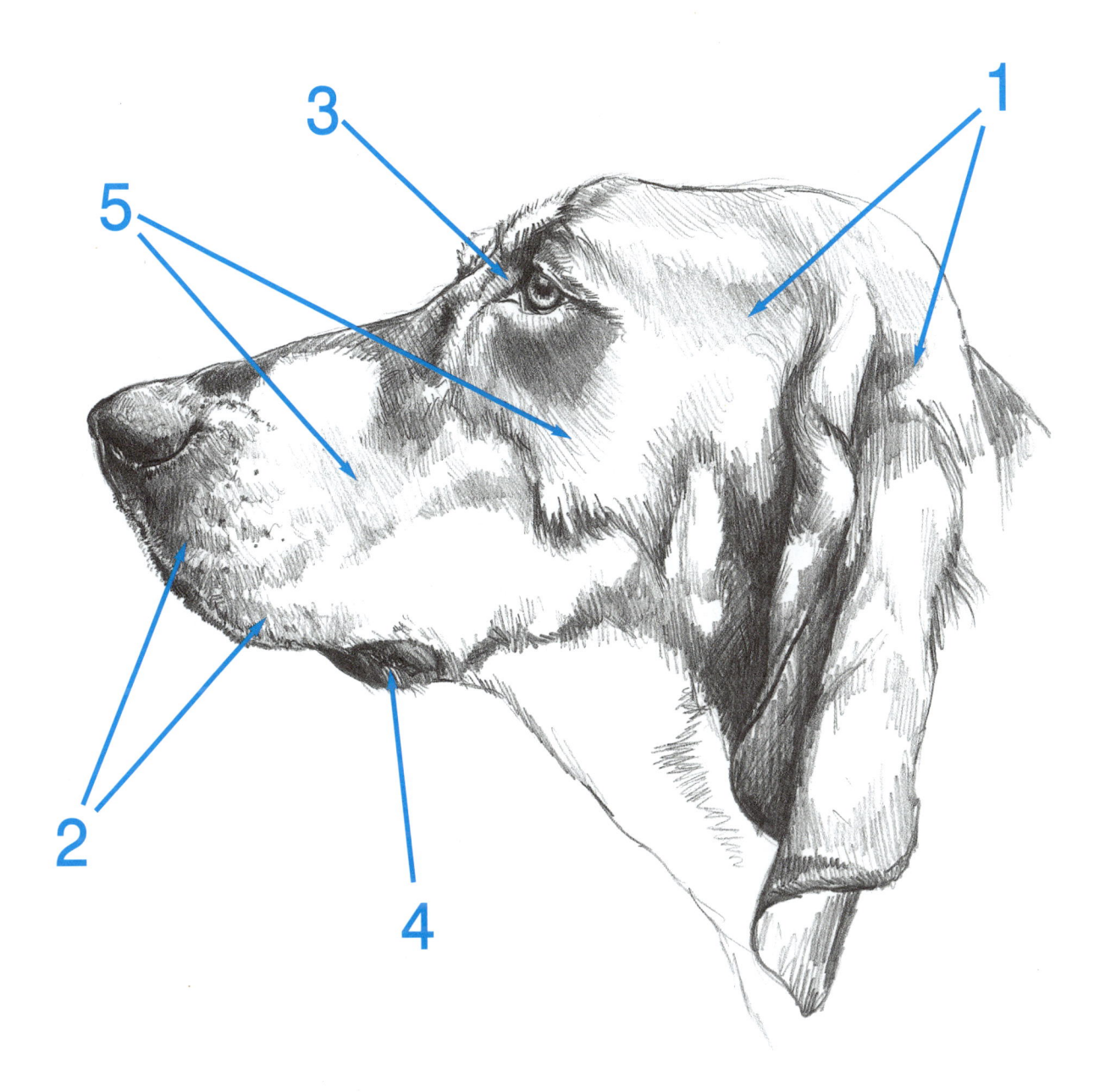

1. With a 4B pencil, use light strokes to create the hair around the face. Draw softly as too harsh it will make the illustration appear flat and the face will have limited muscle definition.
2. Shade where the freckles fall with a medium tone, helping accentuate shadows around the dimples and whiskers.
3. Keep rendering to a minimum above and around the eye. By leaving the lower eyelid mainly white, this area becomes a highlight and leaves the focus on details within the eye.
4. The part of the mouth where the folds of skin protrude should remain dark, contrasting the rest of the muzzle. This also assists with the "hound dog look" and makes his expression more serious and ponderous.
5. Little detail is required for the fur on the muzzle and cheeks. The rendering should be light with just a slight suggestion as to the dogs markings and where the muscles lay beneath the skin.

Drawing Dogs

DALMATIAN

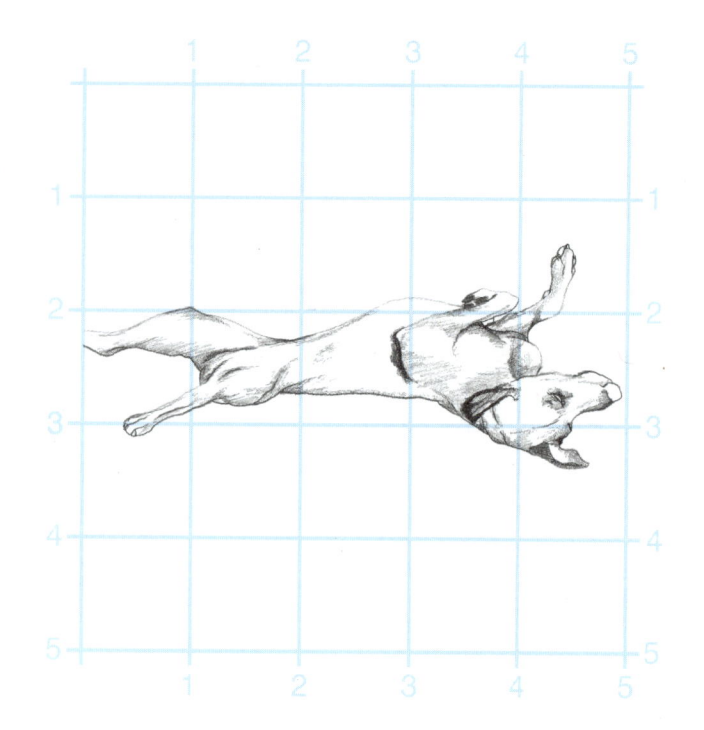

STEP 1:
Use a 2B pencil to draw the outline and details of the dog. Follow the example by creating the main features, as depicted within the finished sketch. When this stage is reached you may need to erase any unnecessary lines or mistakes.

STEP 2:
Using a 4B and a 6B pencil to lightly render the image, copy the techniques shown in the example and read the observation details to help achieve an accurate result.

Drawing Dogs

OBSERVATION DETAILS:

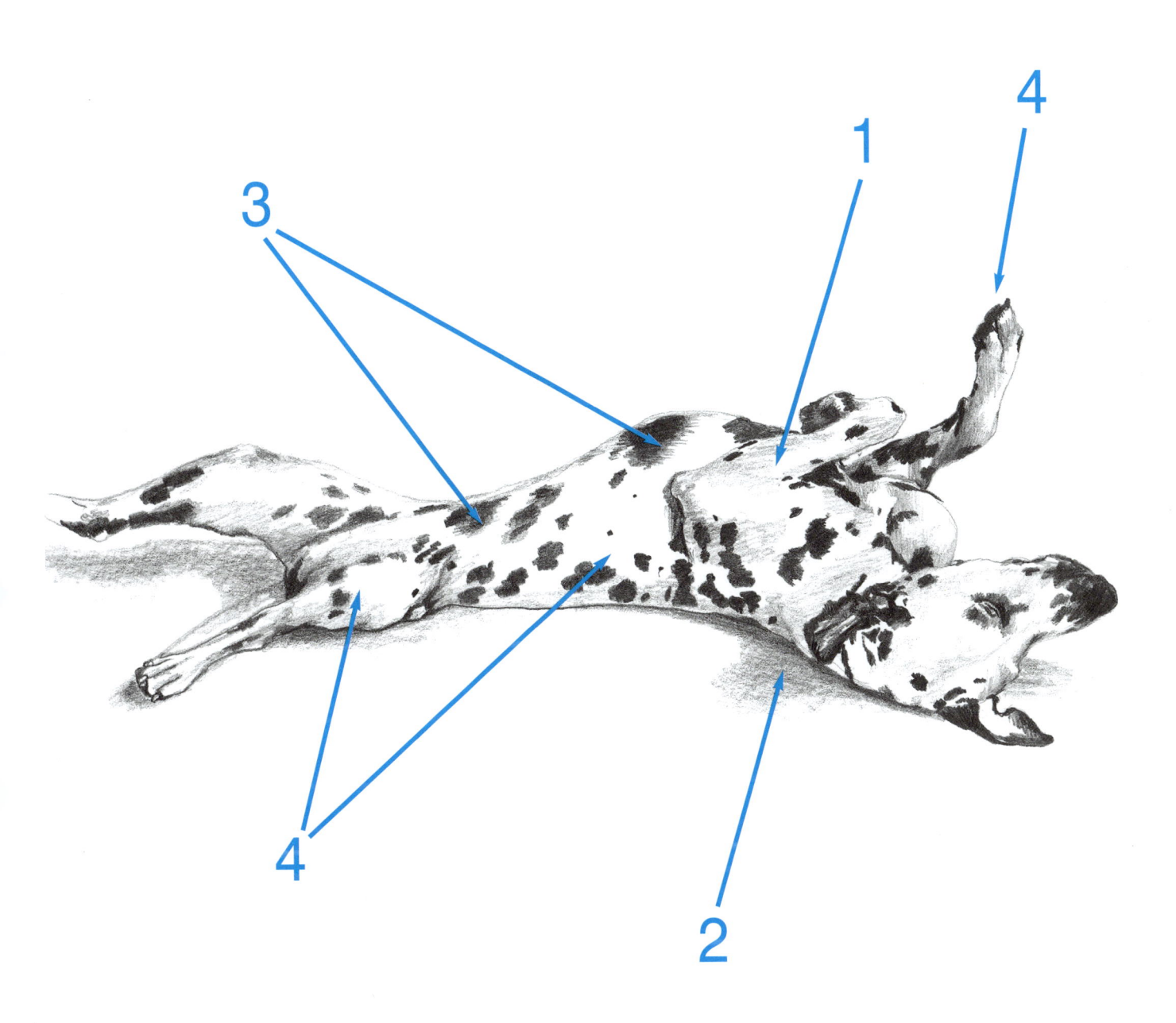

1. Without filling in the surface area along the dog's body too extensively, keep shadows to a minimum and shade only to show muscle definition.
2. Using a similar depth of shading for the floor shadow, will accentuate and compliment the dogs position, without dominating. The shadows darkest area should be that which is closest to the body and fades away as it extends across the floor.
3. The spots on the Dalmatian should not be drawn too solidly, as this will reduce the sense of fur and appear too flat. Keeping the edges rough Dogs curved with the form of the body.
4. The proportions and angles of the chest, legs and pelvis need to be correct, without this the body will seem distorted. Note the thigh closest to the viewer appears smaller than the others. This is called fore-shortening and can be difficult when drawing. It does however give the illusion that the dog is close and seemingly three dimensional.

Drawing Dogs

CAVALIER KING CHARLES SPANIEL

STEP 1:
Use a 2B pencil to draw the outline and details of the dog. Follow the example by creating the main features, as depicted within the finished sketch. When this stage is reached you may need to erase any unnecessary lines or mistakes.

STEP 2:
Using a 4B and a 6B pencil to lightly render the image, copy the techniques shown in the example and read the observation details to help achieve an accurate result.

Drawing Dogs

OBSERVATION DETAILS:

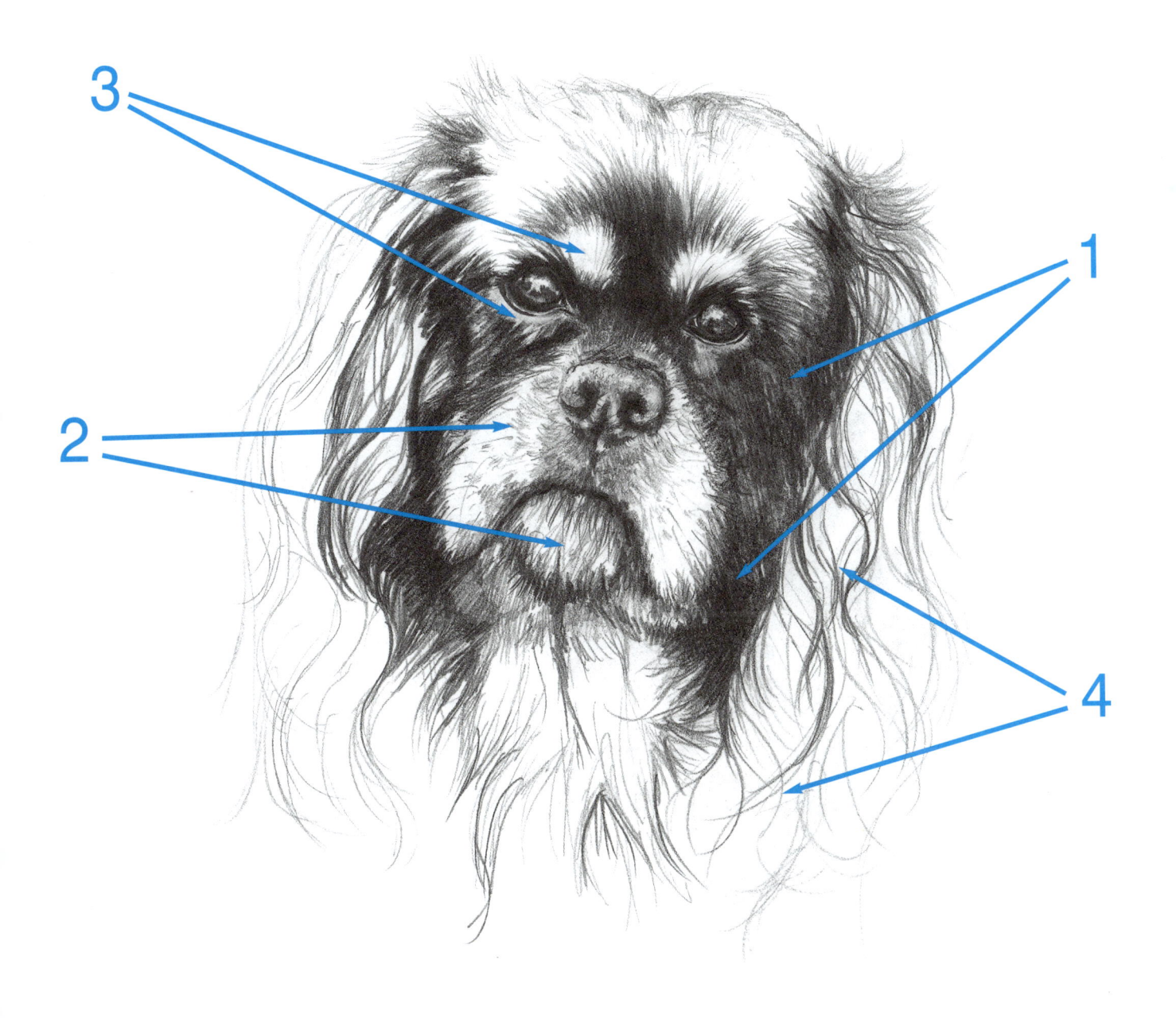

1. Fully render the facial area, leaving the ears and chest in line with a few darkened areas to suggest shadow. This enhances eyes, nose and muzzle which then become main focal points of the composition.

2. The nose, jowls and chin need to be much lighter than the rest of the face, making this section appear more pronounced and three dimensional. If not they will become lost in the shading.

3. The eyebrows and areas under the eyes need to be basically white, with little or no rendering. The contrast draws the viewers attention to the Spaniel's eyes, which are dark and full of expression.

4. The Cavalier King Charles Spaniel has lovely wavy fur on it's ears and body, which is challenging fun to draw. Practise getting the correct depth of this wavy fur without making it overly neat. Each strand of fur should flow in roughly the same direction and follow the length of the ears. Although if it is too orderly, the wavy effect will be lost.

Drawing Dogs

GERMAN SHEPHERD

STEP 1:
Use a 2B pencil to draw the outline and details of the dog. Follow the example by creating the main features, as depicted within the finished sketch. When this stage is reached you may need to erase any unnecessary lines or mistakes.

STEP 2:
Using a 4B and a 6B pencil to lightly render the image, copy the techniques shown in the example and read the observation details to help achieve an accurate result.

Drawing Dogs

OBSERVATION DETAILS:

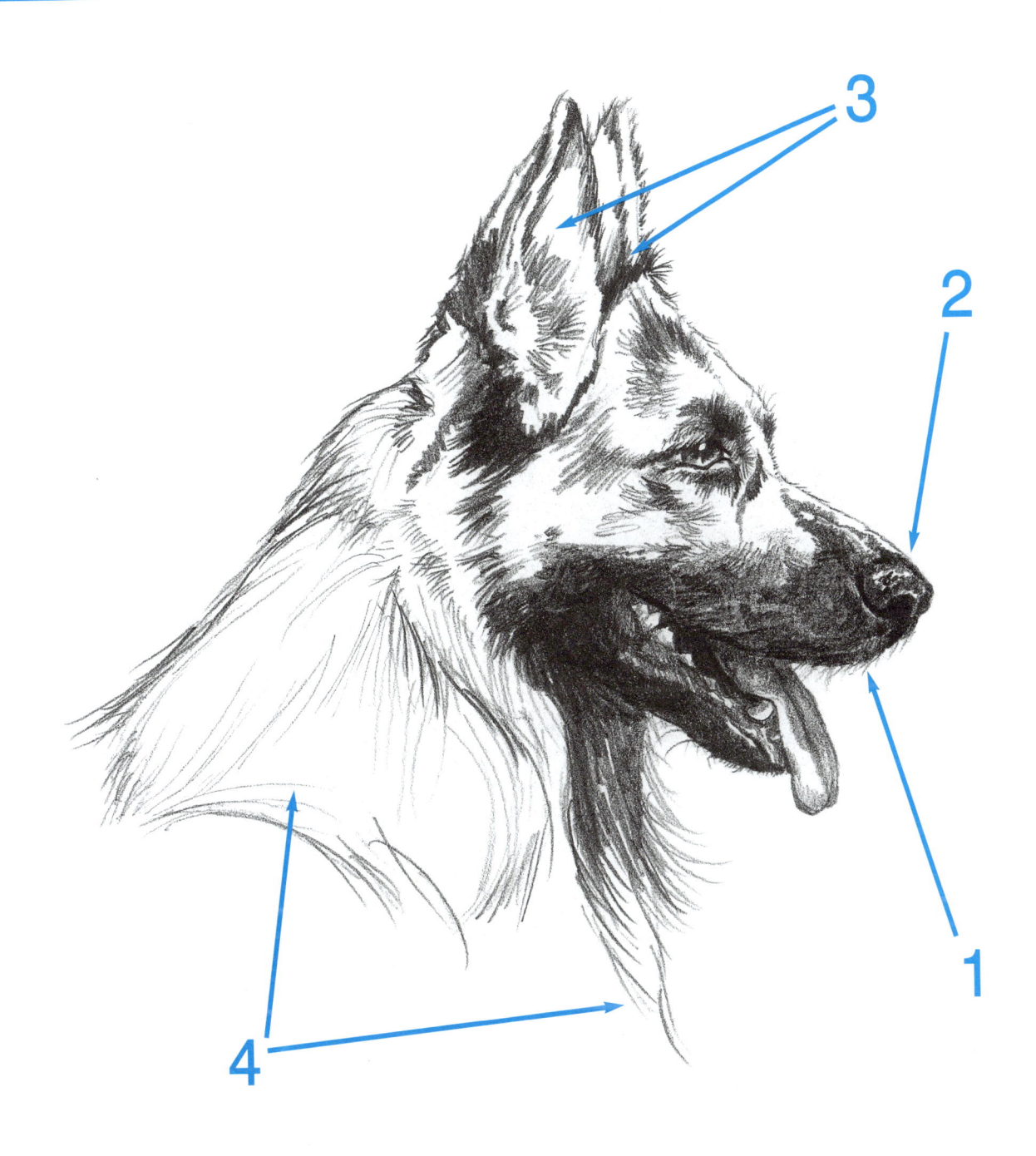

1. The German Shepherd's muzzle consists of rather dark fur and can be drawn while retaining control of the rendering technique. Do not be tempted to solidly shade across this area, as loss of texture and detail will occur. Be aware not to overlap your strokes into white areas.
2. Similarly, the black nose can be roughly shaded to develop texture. The reflections will keep the look of moisture and distinguish the nose from the rest of the black muzzle.
3. The ears being quite furry, can be effectively achieved by using gentle strokes in an outward motion. Use a flicking action at the end to taper the line. Keep the strokes in a regular pattern, whilst varying a few here and there, giving it more movement.
4. To finish your composition, show a few sketch lines of fur along the chest. Just a few strokes should be ample to suggest the direction of the thick fur on the neck and chest.

Drawing Dogs

BASSET HOUND

STEP 1:

Throughout this book, you have learnt to visualise, capture proportions and render accurately your image. Once drawing with confidence, focus on this image and then try to recreate using all the techniques mastered.

Drawing Dogs

OBSERVATION DETAILS:

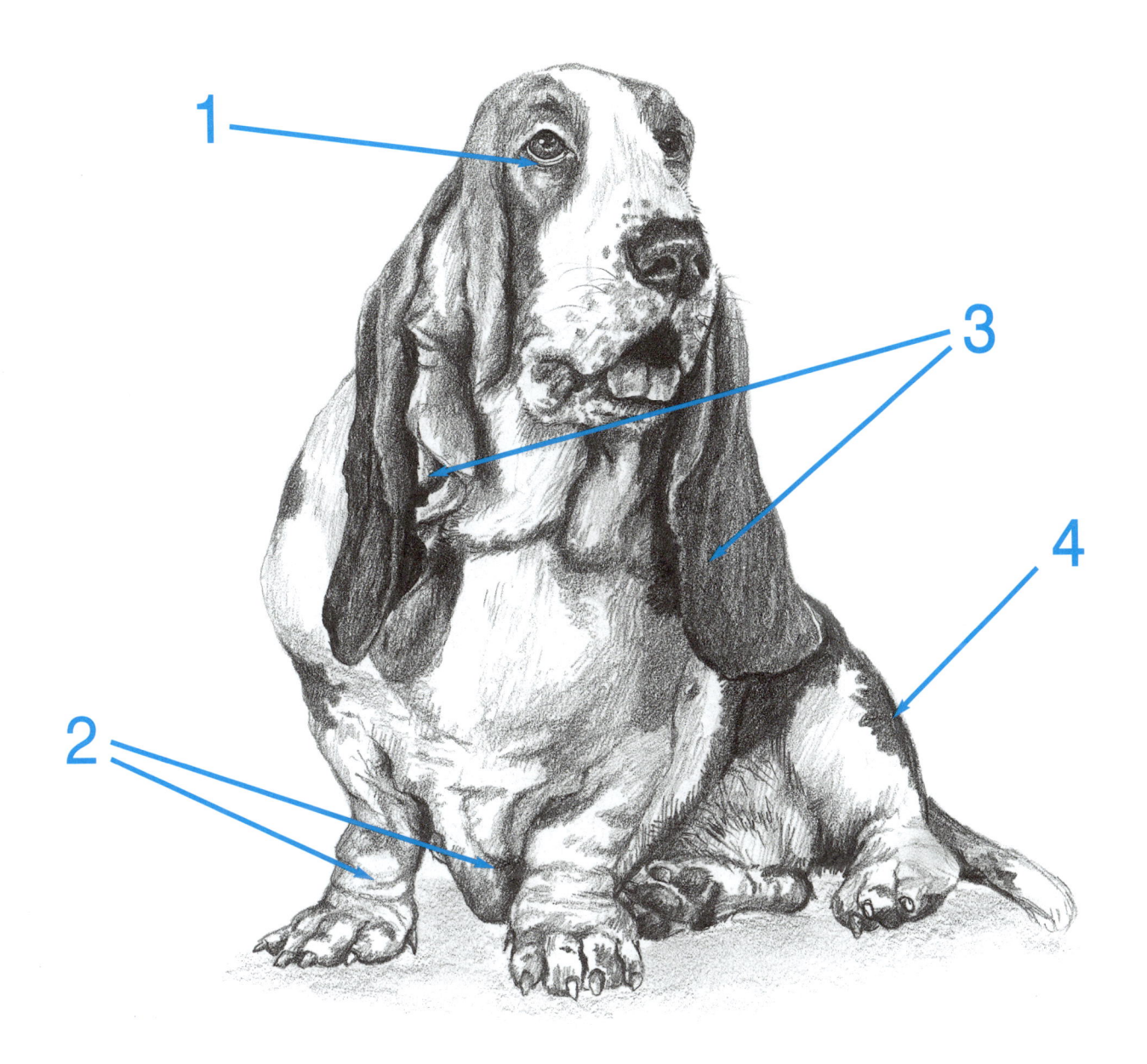

1. The Basset Hound's eyelids droop to reveal more of the eyeball and membrane than usual. As a main trait of this breed, to emphasise, it should remain white.
2. The Basset Hound has large, heavy paws and saggy skin which collects around the ankles and rest of the body. Special attention should be given to the folds of skin, as although they need to be shown, the skin is predominately white with little colouring. Draw the toe nails accurately, as these help accentuate the angle of each toe.
3. The Hound's ears are extra large, long and hang well below the jaw line. Note the way in which they fold about the head. This is where each highlight becomes pertinent in defining the detail of the fur, as well as the crinkles.
4. Patches of colour in amongst the white along the dog's body, must have a different look to that of the shadowed areas. They should be rendered at a similar tone and have a moderately hard edge to them, without being outlined.

Drawing Dogs

DOG BREED DESCRIPTIONS

To best capture the essence and character of your subject, as well as develop as an artist, a study and understanding of your choice of subject is most important. Here is a short description of the dog breeds covered in this book. There are brief explanations only and it is recommended a more extensive study be made for greater understanding of the breed itself.

PUG
A short and robust little character with a lively personality. Once companions of Buddhist monks, they were developed from the original Mastiff. They are very sociable, good-natured and make loving members of the family.

MIXED BREED
These wonderfully loyal companions have interesting backgrounds and come in a variety of colours, sizes and shapes. They often derive from a mixture of breeds, therefore recognising their heritage can be difficult. Often however, there are distinguishing features which may identify a certain breed or two.

GOLDEN RETRIEVER
The Retriever is well known for it's beautiful, relaxed, puppy-like temperament. They often work with people as Guide Dogs for the Blind and as Explosives/Drug Detectors. The breed was developed in Britain in the late 19th Century.

AFGHAN HOUND
The Afghan is an ancient breed, acknowledged by the western world in the 19th Century. The Afghan is glamourous with its long, silky, elegant coat and athletic frame. They have boundless energy and were once hunting dogs in the mountains of Afghanistan. His expression is superior and dignified, his personality is commonly known to be eccentric and playful.

WEIMARANER
The Weimaraner is an excellent dog with a friendly personality. They enjoy running and regular exercise and have a puppy-like nature. Possibly their most distinctive feature is their piercing amber or blue-grey eyes.

AIREDALE TERRIER
The Airedale originates from Northern England and is the largest of all the terriers. The breed can be stubborn, although generally intelligent with a laughing expression on an impressively bearded face. Their coat is short with a strong wave to the fur.

Drawing Dogs

BULLDOG
The Bulldog has a short coat which can be all manner of colours. They are a massively built dog, yet they have a quiet nature and can be rather stubborn. They adore children and are very appealing, due to their comical pushed-in noses and upturned chin.

BULL TERRIER
The Bull Terrier is known as 'the gladiator of the terriers', due to his burly figure and reputation as a fighter. White is the primary colour for the Bull Terrier, however they can have coloured markings on the head featuring black, red, fawn and brindle. The Bull Terrier is an active dog with a short flat coat.

DACHSHUND
Dachshunds can come in six different varieties, all of which are similar in shape, being low to the ground and long in the body. They were bred to hunt and chase badgers and other animals, yet they have very affectionate personalities.

PEKINGESE
Loyal, courageous and fierce in the defence of its owner, the small Pekingese is highly valued for its strong personality. For centuries Pekingese were favoured in the Imperial Palace, Beijing.

SILKY TERRIER
The Silky Terrier is a breed full of character, with a beautifully long, straight coat. Silkies may have been bred primarily as companion dogs for the home, but they are also great rat-catchers.

SIBERIAN HUSKY
The Siberian Husky is a sled dog reminiscent of a wolf but with a more kindly expression. This breed is keenly alert and rarely lowers its ears. Their eyes are remarkable because of their piercing clarity and can vary to the extent that they can even possess one blue and one brown eye. The Husky coat is densely thick, protecting them from a cold, snowy climate.

LABRADOR
The Labrador is thought to have originated from Greenland. They are a stockily built dog famous for their stamina. A favourite family pet and similar to the Golden Retriever in their nature and skills.

Drawing Dogs

WEST HIGHLAND WHITE TERRIER
This breed is affectionately known as the 'Westie'. An inquisitive outlook and great courage make the West Highland Terrier an invaluable guard dog and member of the family. A popular breed due to this outgoing manner and love of people. The Westie has a happy expression and loves attention.

BLACK & TAN COONHOUND
These dogs are descendants of the Foxhound and the Bloodhound and were bred in the United States. They are well known for their ability to endure extreme weather conditions. They are powerful, alert and friendly in their attitude towards people.

DALMATIAN
A distinctive breed made famous in the Disney Classic "101 Dalmatians". Having either black or red-brown coloured spots on their white bodies. The friendly Dalmatian loves to exercise and no part of them is ever still, especially their long tapering tail.

CAVALIER KING CHARLES SPANIEL
These are pretty little dogs, which make wonderful companions. With an impressive appetite they love to go on walks, play and require plenty of affection. Known as "toy dogs", they are a popular breed.

GERMAN SHEPHERD
German Shepherds are powerful and strong, making them loyal companions. They are intelligent, respond well to training and are often used as guard dogs. Bred by German monks who needed to protect their monasteries from bandits.

BASSET HOUND
The loveable Basset Hound, originally from France, is a slow moving, ponderous pack hound originally used for hunting the hare. Having a great character and a cheerful disposition, even if their facial expressions could be described as "sad". They come in colours of black, white and tan, or lemon and white.